A TREE GROWS IN
LINCOLN

A TREE GROWS IN LINCOLN

A History of Christ Temple Mission Church

ARTHUR L. LINDSAY

A TREE GROWS IN LINCOLN
A HISTORY OF CHRIST TEMPLE MISSION CHURCH

iUniverse books may be ordered through booksellers or by contacting:

iUniverse
1663 Liberty Drive
Bloomington, IN 47403
www.iuniverse.com
1-800-Authors (1-800-288-4677)

ISBN: 978-1-4917-4293-8 (sc)
ISBN: 978-1-4917-4292-1 (hc)
ISBN: 978-1-4917-4291-4 (e)

Library of Congress Control Number: 2014915622

Printed in the United States of America.

iUniverse rev. date: 12/10/2014

CONTENTS

In loving memory of
Trago O. and Margaret McWilliams

Rev Trago & Margaret McWilliams

Dedicated to Eddie Key—the Gentle Giant

Eddie Key

April 4, 1995-February 8, 2014

"Train up a child in the way he is to go,
and when he is old he will not depart from it."
(Proverbs 22:6)

ACKNOWLEDGMENTS

This book is made possible because of the help of many people:

Albert Maxey Sr.—for painting the cover of this book, and for helping raise funds so this commemorative story could come to fruition.

Karen McWilliams—for supplying invaluable information on the McWilliams family heritage.

G. J. Mills —for editing and writing portions of the book

Angela Pillow—for providing photography services

Many past and present Christ Temple members—for sharing their stories

SPECIAL THANK YOU

In 2006, the congregation of Christ Temple Mission was able to move back into their refurbished church building at 500 North 25th Street. Although slated for demolition, this historic building stands today because of the contribution of many.

Stephen May, President & Robert Killeen, Vice President
MCS Church Builders Inc.
Randy K. Meyer, Architect & Louis J. Sobczyk, Project Engineer
Meyer & Associates

Without their initial construction expertise and building plan development of these individuals, the renovation project would not have happened.

———

Charles Berryman & Tim Wentz, Professors
of Construction Management
University of Nebraska
College of Engineering, Durham School of
Architectural Engineering & Construction

Under their guidance, 85 students participated in developing remodeling plans

———

Ross Greathouse, of Greathouse Associates, Ltd. provided the interior design and coordination.

Reverend Dr. Luke Schnacke and the congregation of Christ Lutheran Church assisted Christ Temple Mission Church during the years that the building was being restored. During this time, 18 men from their congregation built an interior wall on the Northside of the structure which prevented a major collapse of the entire building.

Rick Wallace and Jeff Bruenig of the
Community Development Resource
for their many efforts to provide essential financial support.

There are many contractors and individuals who provided materials and labor of love without remuneration and made the remodeling project a reality.

PREFACE

By Alan Jacobsen

When I asked my friend, Art Lindsay, to write a book as a tribute to my spiritual mentor, Trago O. McWilliams, I was serving as the project manager at Christ Temple Mission for the remodeling project. Since that time, I served as Sr. Pastor before stepping down from that position in 2013. I still enjoy teaching Sunday School and filling in at the pulpit when needed. My good friend, John Harris, became Senior Pastor in early 2014.

Art agreed to the undertaking on the condition that the narrative would focus on the spiritual church rather than the refurbished historic structure at 500 North 25th Street. A building is certainly not the congregation. In fact, Trago and his wife, Margaret, founded the church some 30 years prior to moving to the current location in1970.

Any Bible student quickly learns from reading the *Book of Acts* that the early church didn't focus on building projects, but rather the promulgation of the Gospel of Jesus Christ. Interestingly enough however, the renovation process of Christ Temple Mission's red brick edifice serves as a metaphor of the Lord's faithfulness in the Christian journey. Rather than being demolished, the building was restored. The Lord gives "beauty for ashes" (Isaiah 61:3).

The genesis of this book began over a decade ago when I learned that the Christ Temple Mission church building was slated to be torn down. Stunned and heartbroken over the news, I found myself steering my vehicle toward the familiar stomping grounds of my youth.

As I approached the site, it was immediately obvious that the entire north side of the structure was caving in. Six steel beams imbedded in concrete (known as "dead weight" in the Navy) kept the building erect. As I pulled off to the side of the street, I noticed a "For More Information" sign. With a lump in my throat, I quickly jotted down the phone number on a piece of scratch paper.

It seemed somewhat ironic as I drove away, that "dead weight" was upholding the structure that once housed such vibrant life-giving church services. Yet, Scripture teaches that out of death, new life is often brought forth. "Very truly I tell you, unless a kernel of wheat falls to the ground and dies, it remains only a single seed. But if it dies, it produces many seeds." (John 12:24)

Perhaps the best days for Christ Temple Mission were just around the corner.

My hope was short-lived. When I made the call, Reverend Thomas Sadler told me the church members had voted to tear the church down. My inner turmoil intensified throughout the evening and into the night. As I tossed and turned, unable to sleep, it seemed that I heard noise, like the dial of a radio signal between stations. I began to pray for family and friends, but inevitably my thoughts revisited the events of the day. I asked God to give me peace about the jolting news that the Christ Temple Mission Church building was being demolished. I tried to sleep, but the noise continued.

In the twilight hours, it became apparent my burden wasn't lifting. As I wrestled with the Lord in prayer, I began to consider the cost. I've worked in construction most of my life, and I knew that undertaking a commitment to save the building from the wrecking crew would be daunting. My prayer became an argument. "Lord I'm busy with my family and business." The fuzzy noise inside my head continued as my excuses mounted, but God seemed to remain silent.

I finally blurted out, "Lord, I'm in the middle of building my own house and it's not done!" Suddenly, the noise stopped and I heard the still small voice; "and my house is not done either." God was giving me the opportunity to be the catalyst for refurbishing the 100 year-old building. Immediately, the peace that surpasses all understanding overcame me, and I made a commitment to God that I would pursue the project the next day. My heart was quieted as I faded off to sleep.

The next day, I called Reverend Saddler and enthusiastically shared that I had 20 years construction experience and wanted to look at the building to see if there was something that I could do to help. He referred me to the church president, Joan McWilliams. Joan, whose husband, Art, is the nephew of Trago, graciously explained that no one wanted to see the building demolished, but that restoration didn't seem feasible. However, unbeknownst to the members at the time they voted to tear the building down, the church bylaws stipulated that the structure could not be demolished without a unanimous vote.

Church members were also unaware that the University of Nebraska College of Engineering and Technology had undertaken a student project involving Christ Temple Mission. Twelve groups comprised of 85 students from three classes, conducted studies on whether or not the building should be remodeled or demolished. Ultimately, there were four recommendations for demolition, but eight plans were submitted to remodel the building.

After visiting the site and studying the building condition, I concurred that it was salvageable, and subsequently shared my enthusiasm with the church board. Each member was excited and I was asked to provide a building plan. My wife and business partner, Lori, and I both knew that the project was beyond our company's scope of expertise, so we contacted a church builder whom we had worked with on another project.

The estimated cost of the remodeling project was $870,000. Since the church only had $250,000 on hand, the remainder would have to be raised and borrowed. The church board voted to recommend the plan to the congregation during a special meeting.

God moved mightily through the construction company. They went the extra mile and came to the meeting with a brochure, blue prints, and building permit in hand. Usually, the builder doesn't hire an architect or engineer until the contract is signed. The congregation voted unanimously to move forward with the remodeling project and I was identified as the building liaison.

For me, this was a moment of faith and commitment. I wrote to Joan and the congregation, quoting a passage from Nehemiah 2:17-18. "Then I said to them, You see the distress that we are in, how Jerusalem is laid waste, and its gates are destroyed with fire. Come and let us rebuild the wall of Jerusalem and we will no longer be a reproach. And I told them of the hand of God which is good upon me and also of the King's words that he had spoken to me. So I said, let us rise up and let us build! And their hands were strengthened for good work."

The construction company had completed extensive demolition, and installed steel beams and structural bridge trusses. They were paid for the completed work, but had no choice but to resign from the project after the church was unable to secure a loan. At that point, I put pen to paper and estimated that if we were to become our own job superintendent, we could complete the project $380,000 under the original estimate. Even then, we needed an additional $250,000 to finish the project. We were able to secure a loan with some additional collateral from a local donor.

As the project drew to a close, additional funds were needed and once again, God provided a way for the church to secure those funds. All unsecured loans have since been paid back, and on August 5, 2006, we returned to our newly remodeled building.

The building on North 25th Street is merely a conduit for ministry. This book is about the vision of Trago O. McWilliams and the people who have continued his commitment to overcome the racial barrier that divides God's people on Sunday morning.

To fully appreciate Trago's vision, one must understand the times in which he lived. Dr. Martin Luther King, Jr. was only an eleven year old child when Trago and Margaret McWilliams began their interracial congregation in 1940. It's inconceivable now, but reaching across racial lines was radical. Yet, Trago remained true to the Gospel message and instilled in many a faith heritage that in Christ Jesus, followers are neither "Jew nor Greek" (Gal 3:38) —and specifically, in the case of

Christ Temple Mission, neither black nor white nor brown. Dietrich Bonhoeffer writes in *Living Together* that God wants us to live in a "community within a community." Our church is a bastion of hope to anyone who needs refuge from the storms in life.

Christ Temple Mission had already been a beacon in Lincoln for over a quarter of a century when I sat under Trago's tutelage, and the impact was so profound that to this day, his teaching is part of my spiritual DNA. During the 1960s, my parents expanded our family of four boys to include three girls. Adoption was not common in the mid-part of the last century and choosing to adopt children outside of one's race was almost nonexistent. Nonetheless, my Mom and Dad defied convention and our family was blessed to include a sister from Korea and two bi-racial black sisters from local adoption organizations. After experiencing raised eyebrows and even discrimination from various elements within the Christian community, my family found a home in the small, interracial church.

Unfortunately, over 50 years after Martin Luther King, Jr.'s observation in 1963 that the most segregated hour in the country was during Sunday morning service, churches in America remain overwhelmingly racially divided. A recent Barna study found that only 5% to 7.5% of churches in the U.S. are considered to be racially diverse. "Ninety percent of African-American Christians worship in all-black churches. Ninety percent of white American Christians worship in all-white churches," according to Chris Rice, coauthor of *More Than Equals: Racial Healing for the Sake of the Gospel.*

Christ Temple Mission remains true to its founder's original mission, providing people of every color and economic means with a place to come together, worship together and fellowship together—all to the Glory of God. May God bless every person who reads this book, and experience the transforming power of God's grace which is freely given when received by faith, and lived in the hope of His Glory.

INTRODUCTION
By Art Lindsay

It's quite evident! From the time the Almighty Creator first formed man from the dust of the earth, He gave special significance to one plant more than the others. In the middle of the garden that God made for man, He had planted two special trees. One was called simply "the tree of life" and the other "the tree of the knowledge of good and evil" (Genesis 2:9).

The story is all too familiar as to how the evil tempter deceived that first man and his wife and they broke the only law God gave them—a command of obedience. In pride, they ate from the attractive fruit of the tree of knowledge, and broke the intimate relationship they had had with Elohim. Gone was the purity and goodness of man and woman. Now they were locked permanently in the endless difficulty of making choices between good and evil.

Remaining from that horrific story of disobedience is a burgeoning question that begs for an answer: Why was the other tree ignored? Was there nothing of beauty in that tree, nothing appealing or attractive? Was it so plain, yet yearning to offer life to anyone who would come near? Surely this is the Christ about whom Isaiah wrote seven hundred years before Jesus came with the final invitation to life. "He grew up before him like a tender shoot, and like a root out of the ground. He had no beauty or majesty to attract us to him, nothing in his appearance that we should desire him." (Isaiah 53:2)

Why did Satan not encourage man to choose life? That answer is obvious – he is the enemy, not a friend. He is a messenger of darkness, not light. Indeed, he hates the light – as do all those who follow him. "Everyone who does evil hates the light, and will not come into the light for fear that his deeds will be exposed."(John 3:20)

It's interesting that God punished the serpent for being used by the deceiver. And He punished man for giving into the temptation of the evil one. But God did not punish the two trees. In fact, they still stand. Man is faced continually with a choice between them: all the worldly intelligence and success on the one hand, or life by God's terms on the other. So the story of Scripture, from that day to this, is the epoch of how the Lord God Almighty went to great lengths to rescue man from the clutches of evil. "For he has rescued us from the dominion of darkness and brought us into the kingdom of the Son he loves, in whom we have redemption through his blood, the forgiveness of sins." (Colossians 1:13-14)

God has continuously, over the long centuries since that crash to wickedness, maintained a root in His garden that anyone may tap into. "If some of the branches have been broken off, and you, though a wild olive shoot, have been grafted in among the others and now share in the nourishing sap of the rich root of the olive tree." (Romans 11:17)

One piece of God's plan, for the extension of His unique way of salvation for all men through the grace that is in Jesus Christ, was to establish a tree of faith in Lincoln, Nebraska. Its roots had an uncommon strength from the misery suffered for more than several hundred years of slavery. Men and women, bought and sold like cattle – and often treated worse – had to look beyond this world to have any hope at all.

Many found their consolation in Jesus, for they could identify with Him as a "suffering servant". Though their faith in Christ did not change the conditions which they oftentimes endured, He gave them grace and strength to live above their circumstances.

This book looks at the truth of the Gospel message. Through faith in Jesus Christ and the transforming power of the Holy Spirit, believers truly are "more than conquerors."

CHAPTER ONE

The Spiritual Roots of Christ Temple Mission

Before Jesus Christ ascended into Heaven, He assured his followers that the Father was sending a Comforter—a Spirit of truth that would dwell within them (John 14:16-17). Sometimes, believers deny the "still small voice" and follow the traditions of man rather than the heart of God. But for those with listening hearts, the Holy Spirit is able to shine a spotlight into areas of great darkness. Obedience on the part of God's children often leads to blessings and deliverance not just for themselves, but for others as well.

Clearly when Frederick Douglass was converted to Christianity as a young 13 year-old slave in 1831, the Lord was about to use him for a mighty service that would impact the world. Obviously through the power of the Holy Spirit, the young Frederick was able to see that a natural extension of his new life in Christ was to advocate for the liberty of those (including himself) shackled by the chains of slavery.

As a young man the future abolitionist helped establish secret Sunday Schools whereby slaves learned to read by reading the Bible. In 1838, he became a preacher in the African Methodist Episcopal Zion Church in New Bedford, Massachusetts. From early on, Frederick couldn't separate his Christian faith from the need for social reform.

The Holy Spirit doesn't work in a vacuum, and at the same time that the Lord was mightily using Frederick Douglass in Maryland and beyond to advocate for the freedom of all men, spiritual seeds were being planted for a church to spring forth on the Nebraska plains some 100 years before its visible inception.

The story of Christ Temple Mission doesn't begin in 1940 in Lincoln, Nebraska with Trago O. McWilliams. It begins in the heart of God—moving in the hearts of people who had been subjected to the harshest of circumstances. In order to understand the founding pastor's vision, one must know something of the events and people that helped shape his perspective, his paradigm.

It's obvious that the plight and fortitude of the people from whence Trago McWilliams came had a monumental impact in forming his convictions and life's work. One set of his paternal great-great grandparents, Samuel and Phanie True, had 18 living children born into slavery. Samuel was industrious enough to buy himself, his wife, and all of his sons. However, daughters could not be bought since they were deemed as valuable to their masters. One of those daughters was Eliza True, Trago's great grandmother.

According to Eliza, her daughter, Sarah (Trago's grandmother), entered the world around "May-apple time" in 1854 at Iowa Point, Kansas. Eliza, who was deprived of any educational advantages, didn't know exact dates so she connected happenings with the seasons of the year. Mother and daughter were sold, like a cow and a calf, three times; finally to a man in Savannah, Missouri. Here they lived until freedom came, when the mother was turned from the master's door with three children and no place to live.

With dauntless courage, unfailing will power, and an unlimited faith in God, the little mother cared for her children without separating them. When Eliza married a man named Moses Stepney, ten-year-old Sarah was placed with a Baptist deacon and his family in Christian Ridge, Missouri. Here she received the munificent sum of $1.50 per month, and was responsible for the household's laundry, cleaning, cooking, and baking, plus she had to milk twice a day. At night, she was relegated to sleep on a pallet on the third floor, even during the heat of summer and cold of winter.

Sarah had witnessed firsthand the horrors of forced sex on her mother, and she let out a piercing scream when the master of the house tried to fondle her. Convulsed with fear, she ran nearly four miles to seek her mother's advice. Eliza, however, had been trained to obey those in authority and counseled her daughter to return to the deacon's home. Sarah went back with a knife, which she fully intended to use if necessary to prevent being raped.

When the two old main sisters in the house fell sick with a fever, Sarah's workload in the three-story house intensified and the servitude was unbearable. A conversation she overhead where the sisters refused an offer to sit up with them during the night became the catalyst for her departure. "We'll just have Sarah make her pallet here in the hall—she can wait on us." This was the last straw for the exhausted little girl and she hurriedly gathered her few belongings, and ran away to her step-grandmother's home. She secured a job at $1.50 a week working in the same hotel as her grandmother. Sometime later, the deacon was hanged in the Dakotas for selling government lands.

After reaching the exceedingly mature age of 14, she married John Jefferson McWilliams, also a former slave in Missouri. John, a native of West Africa, was sold away from his mother at the tender age of two. He naturally cried from the trauma, only to be permanently scared when his new mistress slammed a bunch of keys on the toddler's forehead.

John was the son of George McWilliams whose master, a Kentuckian had said, "It is as impossible to free the slaves as it is to go up and pull Jesus Christ off His throne." When he saw the inevitable signs of freedom, however, he asked George how in the world he figured to take care of his family, if freed. With a twinkle in his eye, George replied, "I'm taking care of my family and yours too now, so what's to hinder me from keeping up my own alone?"

Seeking to do his part in the war against slavery, the young John McWilliams sought to enlist in the army. The enlistment officer told him he looked too young. Not knowing his real age, McWilliams craftily asked, "How old do I have to be to enlist?"

"You ought to be 17 or 18 anyhow," was the answer.

"Well that's just what I am," came the quick reply.

He then served for two-and-a-half years in Company A, 83rd Regiment, U. S. Colored infantry. Rising to the rank of corporal he was honorably discharged and returned to Missouri.

John and Sarah were married on Christmas Day and began housekeeping in a two-room shack. He sharecropped land and she worked for a boarding house – ironing and cooking large quantities of food to be carried in tubs to the field hands. After 15 years of the most arduous labors by the entire household, and moves to Falls City and then Lincoln, Nebraska, the McWilliams family, which had grown to include four children, lived in an eight-room house with brand new furnishings.

John & Sarah McWilliams

John and Sarah McWilliams were hard workers, but first and foremost they were diligent in pursing their personal relationships with God. Rather than being embittered by the scars of slavery, they were devout Christians, active in sharing the Gospel. Sarah founded the first Women's Christian Federation. On August 16, 1895, they both became ordained as pastors by Quinn Chapel African Methodist Episcopal Church.

The next year, along with Reverend William H. Vanderzee, John and Sarah co-founded the Christian Mission Church. It's providential that in 1896, while Trago's grandparents were instrumental in starting a church destined to provide the spiritual roots of his ministry, his future physical church building, which employs temple-like architecture, was built at 500 North 25th Street by the Vine Congregation Church.

Rev Trago T. & Mrs. McWilliams

Trago's grandparents and Reverend Vanderzee were not in a position to build a church, and for the few years meetings were held at two known locations: 912 Wood Street, and the Northwest Corner of 10th and K. In 1902, the Christian Mission Church moved to a one-story framed building at 1209 South 9th Street.

In 1904 the church moved to 124 North 23rd Street and became known as the Third Christian Church. This was the church of Trago's youth. One can only imagine the profound impact that sitting under the Gospel teaching of his former-slave grandfather had on the lad.

Trago's father, Trago T., was a kind and wise man. He earned a living outside of the church his entire life. As foreman at the Martin Bomber plant at Fort Crook during World War II, he was honored for his meritorious service. Trago, Sr. was civically minded and well respected in the community. He organized the Lincoln Civic and Improvement league, and helped organize the Lincoln Urban League.

Trago, Sr. became an ordained minister in 1922, when Trago was 13. Four years later, in 1926, the congregation literally moved the white frame church structure to 2149 U Street.

Chapter Two

A Preacher of the Word

Preacher of the Word

Born on April 2, 1909 in a house on North 13th Street, Trago McWilliams grew up interacting with people across racial lines. His father advocated for civil rights and was well respected and active in the community. Trago's first encounter with racial prejudice came during his junior year at Lincoln High when his classmates nominated him to be cast as the father in a school play, but his teacher suggested that an "American" would be more appropriate for the role. His mother protested to the school and the matter was settled on the spot.

Trago's parents taught him that out of one's relationship with God, came an understanding of how to be in relationship with others. They also encouraged him to be a lifetime learner. After graduating from Lincoln High School in 1928, he attended the University of Nebraska before transferring to Paul Quinn College in Waco, Texas. Trago married and had a son, Richard, but tragically, his wife succumbed to tuberculosis.

In 1931, he married Margaret and the two made their home in Lincoln. Following in the footsteps of his father and grandfather, Trago O. McWilliams became an ordained minister in 1939. He began his ministry in Fremont at the all black African Methodist Episcopal Church. A year later, however, he would begin building a ministry on the foundation of faith he had inherited from his parents and grandparents.

Trago's vision for an integrated, nondenominational congregation in Lincoln, Nebraska was contrary to all conventional wisdom. At that time Lincoln was still an unequal society racially and less than two percent of the city's population was African-American (only about 2,000). There were no black professionals in the community, blacks could not swim in tax-supported public pools, and they could eat at only a few of the restaurants.

Just as her grandson was beginning his ministry, Sarah McWilliams died in 1940 at the age of 86 years in Lincoln. Trago and Margaret began a congregation and work began on restoring the weathered building on U Street that had been both his grandfather's and father's church. The building had been vacant for a number of years when it because the first official site for the congregation that would later be known as Christ Temple Mission. The church met at this site for the next 28 years.

Although the congregation wasn't large, the members viewed themselves as a mission to the Lincoln community at large. After long deliberation, they chose to name their congregation Christ Temple

Mission. The charter, which was drawn up in 1951, lists Trago and Margaret McWilliams, Merrill and Nina Layman, Zora Adams, and Ermia Davis in the incorporation papers.

In 1970, the property at 2149 U Street was purchased by the City of Lincoln in anticipation of building a north-east radial highway. The projected plan never came to fruition, but the city built a park and named it after Trago's father, Trago T. McWilliams. Desiring to maintain a presence in the same neighborhood, Christ Temple purchased the building at 500 North 25th Street for $12,500 from the First Mennonite Church.

Trago & Margaret on steps of Church

Pastor Trago walked with God, and did not view people by the color of their skin. He tried always to consider the heart-felt needs of others, having an intense desire to build bridges between hard-set opinions, and then encourage others to cross over. "No love, no church," was his often stated contention.

Without being mandated to do so, this part of the Body of Christ was virtually decades ahead of its time. The many later governmental pushes toward integration would come years later. Freedom of expression was the hallmark of the church - emphasized from both the pulpit and the pew, proving that the grace of God shown through Christ Jesus is both full of grace and the equalizing factor of life.

Taking his lead from the Apostle Paul, who worked as a tent maker, Trago worked for the State Department of Labor for over 30 years while he was also pastoring the church. From the outset, the teaching in this fellowship was not based on hollow words and empty philosophy, but by a steady living of the truth. Pastor Trago McWilliams walked the Word of God in his daily life and boldly invited others to follow his lead. The demeanor of his life seemed to give credence to a plaque, which hung on the wall of his home – a quote from Isaiah 49:16. "I will never forget you – I have carved you upon the palm of my hand."

With that as a motto he stood tall, though humble, in an attitude of assurance. Though he was not a man of letters and degrees, he taught the Word of God with eloquence.

Trago was willing to learn from anyone, and he was constantly studying in order to expand his knowledge. In fifty years of leadership, he consistently put grace ahead of every consideration, being quick to forgive and careful to judge fairly. He took to heart James 1:19. "My dear brothers, take note of this: Everyone should be quick to listen, slow to speak, and slow to become angry."

The standard by which this humble man of God made assessments of every situation was based on behavior, not on personalities. Consequently, in order to come to a true judgment, pastor McWilliams resorted to prayer - fervent prayer - or as he would express it, "praying through".

Alan Jacobsen remembers that Trago believed that prayer changes things because he knew that in earnest prayer, people are brought together on equal terms. "To him, prayer was not a way to hammer at an opponent, but a means by which God can manifest His will." Trago often quoted Deuteronomy 4:7. "What other nation is so great as to have their gods near them the way the Lord our God is near us whenever we pray to him?"

In citing such a passage he would observe that the word is "pray" not "prey". He insisted that friends of God do not prey on one another. Instead, his emphasis was on the assurance of Jesus in John 12:32. "But I, when I am lifted up from the earth, will draw all men to myself."

The sincerity of his heart was an overwhelming influence to all who sat under his ministry of teaching the Word. For nearly fifty years his clear understanding of the truth of the Scriptures was transferred to the hearts and minds of the congregation in a simple, yet forceful style.

During those years of leadership he preached at least one time with a text from nearly every book in the Bible, which means that those who listened to him received a broad understanding of God's message to His people. Pastor Trago chose to speak more from the book of Psalms than from any other Bible reference, which points toward the fact that he was a loving pastor, wanting to use the power of the consolation of that rich poetry.

His second book of choice was the Gospel of John, which indicates he was evangelical in his approach - wanting people to come to a transforming knowledge of Christ. And his third favorite book for a text was Romans, signifying that he wanted his hearers to have a reasoned approach to what they believed and why. Only on a rare occasion did he develop a topic and proof-text it from Scripture. Rather he was an expositor – taking a text and developing truth from it. His method of preparation was uncomplicated; using whatever notebook paper was available at the moment he sat down to contemplate a message.

Trago McWilliams judged the merits of every sermon he preached on this special standard. He wanted no attention for himself, only desiring to point men and women and boys and girls to the Savior of all mankind. He had a unique way in which to highlight a particular thought. He would pause and say, "By way of parenthesis"; then strike his listeners with a salient point. After one of his many inspiring sermons on a Sunday morning, one of the members observed, "Trago was as bold as love!" This is what was truly characteristic of the man, because he consistently emphasized that love is the greatest gift of all. Referring to 1 Corinthians 12:3 a, he would often say, "If you are going to seek a gift, seek the gift of love."

Fortunately, hundreds of his sermon notes survived him, folded and tucked away in a cardboard box and a paper grocery sack. The inspiration within them causes even the most casual reader to pause and contemplate the depth of this man's understanding of what the Holy Spirit intended as He led men to put the Scriptures down in black and white. Written in a flowing script, Pastor Trago's notes reveal the heart of a man who loved his Lord and his people and sought to bring the two of them together through the exposition of God's holy Word. There never was a nursery, so children grew up listening to the teaching of God's Word on Sunday morning. Trago didn't just read Scriptures. He gave a thorough explanation, so that even the youngest ones could gain an understanding of the truth about Jesus. Along with his notes, he packed in illustrations and humor as he preached.

The following four sermon outlines are representative of what the congregation feasted on under the ministry of Trago O. McWilliams. This man truly was a man who walked intimately with God, and imparted the knowledge of the Holy Scriptures to his flock.

Trago Ministry in Action

Trago McWilliams' Sermon Outlines

Blessings of God's Word

Text: Psalm 119:2
> "Blessed are they that keep His testimonies and that seek Him with their whole heart."

I.   Enlivening in content—the Word exposes us to what we really are. Hebrews 4:12 – For the Word of God is quick and powerful, and sharper than any two edged sword, piercing even to the dividing asunder of soul and spirit, and of the joints and marrow, and is a discerner of the thoughts and intents of the heart.

II. Enlightening in operation
     Psalm 19:7-8 – The law of the Lord is perfect, converting the soul; the testimony of the Lord is pure, making wise the simple. The statutes of the Lord are right, reviving the heart; the commandment of the Lord is pure, enlightening the eyes.

III. Enhancing in substance
     1 Peter 1:23 – Being born again; not of corruptible seed, but of incorruptible, by the Word of God, which lives and abides forever.

IV. Emancipating in ministry
John 8:32 – And you shall know the truth, and the truth shall set you free.

V. Enabling in effect—Make them pure and holy through teaching them your words of truth.
John 17:17 – Sanctify them through the truth; your Word is truth.

VI. Embracing in authority
Luke 4:32-36 – And they were astonished at His doctrine; for His word was with power. And in the synagogue there was a man, which had a spirit of an unclean devil and cried out with a voice, saying, "Let us alone: what have we to do with you, Jesus of Nazareth? Have you come to destroy us? I know who you are: the Holy One of God." And Jesus rebuked him saying, "Hold your peace and come out of him." And when the devil had thrown him in the midst, he came out of him, and hurt him not. And they were all amazed, and spoke among themselves, saying, "What a Word is this! For with authority and power he commands the unclean spirits, and they came out."

Jeremiah 23:29 – "Is not my Word like a fire," declares the Lord, "and like a hammer that breaks a rock in pieces?"

VII. Encouraging in promise
2 Peter 1:4 – Through these he has given us his very great and precious promises, so that through them you may participate in the divine nature and escape the corruption in the world caused by evil desires.

Promises eternal – kept in heaven – pure – undefiled – beyond the reach of change and decay.

How Truly Human Was Jesus

Text – John 4:6
> "Jesus therefore being wearied with his journey, sat down
> by the well."

To him a long walk brought weariness; His weariness needed rest;
to rest he sat down by the well.

How worn was his humanity? He was more weary than the disciples. He
had a greater mental strain than they. He had a weariness they knew not of.

His self denials were even then remarkable.

Jesus would in all points be made like unto his brethren.

Jesus would not exempt himself from fatigue.

Jesus would not work a miracle for his own refreshment.

Jesus would not refuse to bear the heat, thirst, or exhaustion.

Jesus has thus made himself able to sympathize with the traveler
who rests by the roadside.

The laborer who is worn out with toil.

The sufferer who feels pain in bone and flesh.

The poor man who must rest on a curb-stone and look for
refreshment to the public water fountain.

The weary mind oppressed by life's long way, which has no
luxurious comfort prepared for it, but finds a measure of repose in
the simple arrangements of nature.

I.   Let your conscience draw a spiritual picture of your wearied Savior.
   1. Jesus is wearied with the sins of the people.
      Isaiah 43:24 – "You have brought me no sweet cone with honey or
      lavished on me the fat of your sacrifices. But you have burdened
      me with your sins and wearied me with your iniquities."

   2. Jesus is wearied with formal worship.
      Isaiah 1:14 – "Your new moons and your appointed feasts my
      soul hates: they are a trouble to me; I am weary to bear them."

3. Jesus is weary with our resistance of His Spirit.
   Isaiah 63:10 – But they rebelled and vexed His Holy Spirit, therefore he turned to be their enemy, and he fought against them.

4. Jesus is weary of the erring through unbelief.
   Psalm 95:10 – "Forty years long was I grieved with this generation, and said it is a people that do err in their heart, and they have not known my ways."

   No wonder Isaiah asks the grave question in chapter 7:13 – And he said, "Hear now, you house of David! Is it a small thing for you to weary men, but will you weary my God also?"

II. Now for a spiritual picture of your waiting Savior.
   1. Jesus waits for comers to the well that He might bless. Men have errands; they come to the well only to draw water, but Christ meets them with his greater errand – salvation.
   2. Jesus waits for the most sinful.
      She had five husbands.

   3. Jesus waits to enlighten, convince and convert.
   4. He waits to accept and commission.
   5. He waits to begin by one convert the in-gathering of a great harvest of souls, as in the call of the Samaritans.
      How long has Jesus waited for you?

III. Let your persistence draw another picture.
   1. Are you not weary of sin and worldliness?
   2. Sit down on the well of your Lord's gracious ordinances.
   3. Wait and watch till Jesus comes.
   4. Ask him for a drink. He has the water of life.
   5. Drink yourselves of the living water, then run to tell others.
      Jesus therefore being wearied of his journey sat down by the well.

Be Spiritually Minded

Text: Romans 8:5-9

> Those who live according to the sinful nature have their minds set on what that nature desires; but those who live in accordance with the Spirit have their minds set on what the Spirit desires. The mind of sinful man is death, but the mind controlled by the Spirit is life and peace; the sinful mind is hostile to God. It does not submit to God's law, nor can it do so. Those controlled by the sinful nature cannot please God. You, however, are controlled not by the sinful nature but by the Spirit, if the Spirit of God lives in you. And if anyone does not have the Spirit of Christ, he does not belong to Christ.

By carnal mind we mean fleshly, that which is not renewed. The result of that depravity which has been transmitted from the first fallen man to all posterity, and this carnal mind is the opposite of the mind as it originally came from the hands of God, when he made man in uprightness.

I.   The carnal mind.
      Once intelligent, now ignorant – once holy, now impure – once happy, now miserable – once bearing the image of the heavenly, now the image of the earthly.

The fruits of the carnal mind:

> Enmity against God, not subject to the law of God - aversion and dislike to God, dislike to the law of God, disobedient, rebellious.
> Dislike to the ordinances of God, to His services, to His day, to hearing His Word, prayer, and praise.
> Dislike to His people. Do not love them because they are not of the world – "The world hates you"

Dislike to the Spirit of God. Quench His Holy emotions, grieve Him. A total enmity, a constant enmity.

Thus to be spiritually minded is death and there is a spiritual death now!

Dead in trespasses and sins.

Insensible to others, unwilling even to avoid the appearance of evil.

II. To be spiritually minded is life and peace. The mind is renewed by The Spirit, born of the Spirit, led by the Spirit, delighting in spiritual things and pursuing spiritual things. Life of faith in Christ and to Christ.

Holy obedience – life of hope – title to eternal life. Peace with God – peace of conscience and peace with all men. Everlasting life – spiritual life perpetuated and consummated in heaven.

You must be born again. Naturally depraved – regeneration is necessary. Nothing will repair or amend it. It must be made entirely new.

Happy and safe are the children of God who are spiritually minded.

Now we must measure up spiritually – be too high to be low: Colossians 3:2 – Set your affections on things above, not on things on earth.

Today's world is overrun by low morals. Sensuality in TV, radio and magazines is the order of the day. God will judge the wicked.

III. We must keep our goals and morals high
Colossians 3:5-6 – Put to death, therefore, whatever belongs to your earthly nature: sexual immorality, impurity, lust, evil desires and greed, which is idolatry. Because of these the wrath of God is coming.

Being spiritually minded we must look for good in others, inspiring them to reach for the best.

1 Peter 3:15 – But sanctify the Lord God in your hearts: and be ready always to give an answer to every man that asks you a reason of the hope that is in you with meekness and fear.

Being spiritually minded is life and peace

Hymn: *Something Within*

1. *Preachers and teacher would make their appeal*
   Fighting as soldiers on great battlefields.
   When to their pleadings my poor heart did yield.
   All I could say, there is something within.

   Something within me that holdeth the reins,
   Something within me that banishes pain,
   Something within me I cannot explain,
   All that I know there is something within.

2. *Have you that something, that burning desire?*
   Have you that something that never doth tire?
   Oh, if you have it – that heavenly fire.
   Then let the world know there is something within.
   Chorus

3. *I met God one morning, my soul feeling bad*
   Heart heavy-laden with a bowed down head.
   He lifted my burden and made me so glad.
   All that I know, there is something within.

   Chorus

Psalm 57:7 – My heart is fixed O God, my heart is fixed; I will sing and give praise.

Ezekiel 36:26 – A new heart also will I give you and a new spirit will I put within you.

Door – Means of Access to Something
(A Rare Topical Message)

Text: John 10:9
> "I am the door; whoever enters through me will be saved. He will come in and go out, and find pasture."

Some notable doors or gates

1. Door of the Ark – Genesis 6:16 – the entrance into the once place of safety from the coming flood.
2. Door of the Tabernacle – Exodus 27:16 and 29:4 – the entrance into the Court and the Holy Places.
3. Door to the City of Refuge – Joshua 20:4 – into which the man slayers fled for refuge.
4. Door of Mercy – Luke 13:25 – Opened in the day of grace, but which one day the Lord will shut.
5. Door of the Sepulcher – Matthew 27:60 – from which the stone had been rolled away when Christ rose from the dead.
6. Great and Effectual Door – 1 Corinthians 16:9 – one of service.
7. Opened for the Gospel a door of utterance – Colossians 4:3 – freedom and power.
8. Open Door – set before the servant of God – Revelations 3:8.
9. Door of the Heart – Revelations 3:20 – before which the Lord stands knocking for admission.
10. Door of Faith opened to the Gentiles – Acts 14:27.
11. Door in Heaven – Revelations 4:1, Revelations 7:14 – into which the righteous enter, who have washed their robes and made them which it the blood of the Lamb.

The door has two sides – outside and inside. One must be either within to enjoy what is there, or outside to be excluded from the privileges and blessings.

Only One Door, and yet its sides are two.
Outside or inside – on which side are you?

CHAPTER THREE

The Little Minister

Margaret & Trago McWilliams

When she was born on November 10, 1910, in Minneapolis, Minnesota, Margaret Stephens was an unlikely prospect to be part of a fruitful spiritual tree in Lincoln, Nebraska. Her mother died before her first birthday and she was sent to live with her grandparents. Her father then served in World War I. When he returned he had fallen victim shell shock, having been stationed just a mile from the incessant bombardment of the German lines – and the American response with heavy cannon fire. When Margaret was ten, she was sent to live with an aunt in Omaha. Then after her father remarried and began working for the university, she was reunited with him in Lincoln.

Always of a vivacious nature, Margaret fit in well at Lincoln High and had a host of friends who did everything together. Among the group was a handsome young man named Trago. After graduation Trago married another girl in the troupe of friends and they soon had a son, Richard. But when the boy was a year old, his mother died.

At Christmas time in 1930 Margaret and Trago met again at a dance. Shyly he asked her, "Could I take you out?" She agreed, but he also had to get permission from her father. Her dad, seeing something special in the young man, readily agreed to the courtship. Just a year later, December 28, 1931, the couple married. Trago supported them by doing janitorial work and other odd jobs, and then finally got a good position with the state Department of Labor. Although he continued to work for the state for over three decades, he was eventually allowed to accommodate his ministerial duties and conduct hospital visits and officiate funerals as the need arose.

In the early days of their marriage, neither Margaret nor Trago was satisfied, because they did not have God as s vital part of their lives. Trago certainly knew better because of the emphasis of Christ in the lives of his grandparents and his father, but he had not yet submitted himself to God. And Margaret loved him so much that she was content to follow Trago in whatever he wanted.

All of that changed, however, when they were invited to attend a revival meeting at Quinn Chapel. The outstanding preaching of the evangelist, a woman named Versa Flynn, challenged both of them. Purposefully they watched the lifestyles of the people in the congregation and were impressed with what they saw. By the time the meetings ended, both of them were converted and began to focus on what God wanted to accomplish in their lives.

Trago jumped into his relationship with Jesus Christ with his whole heart and began to apply himself arduously to the study of the Scriptures. As a result in 1939 he was ordained in the African Methodist Episcopal Church. Later, another all black denomination, the Church of Christ Holiness, also recognized him for ordination. He was greatly used of God in the ministry of the church because he was a very gifted preacher and people knew that he cared deeply for their spiritual welfare. Margaret was a perfect helpmate to her husband, applying her talents with music as an organist, and also in teaching Sunday school.

Nonetheless, they knew that there was something of great importance missing in their lives. They were not content in being partitioned off from their many white friends every Sunday. The black churches were very black. There were no whites in the congregation. Trago and Margaret wanted a church where everyone would be welcome. "If you can't receive one another unconditionally," he said, "you've missed the conversion experience."

Consequently, in 1940, building on the faith of Trago's father and grandfather before him, they launched out to establish a church that would eventually be called Christ Temple Mission. They intently sank their roots deep in that fellowship, intending never to move from the foundation that all men are created equal. The little tree, planted in love and nurtured by the faithful concern of this man and his wife, began to grow.

Though there were many men who came alongside Trago to share in the preaching and teaching, he consistently and lovingly referred to his wife Margaret as the "Little Minister", because they shared the vision and carried the burden for its fulfillment together. Trago was the man in the pulpit and the one seemingly in authority, but he and his wife were always a team, encouraging and challenging one another. Often they would talk late into the night and pray together in unity for the many needs of individuals in the congregation of which only they were aware. People recognized the pastor's wife as someone of significance and spoke of her reverently as "Sister Margaret" and as the years passed, "Mother Margaret".

Trago selected his sermon topics by keeping his ear peeled to the needs of the congregation. "I pay a lot of attention to what people are talking about," he said. "I try to catch the yearning of their hearts. That becomes the topic for my sermon after I've prayed about it. We're supposed to feed the sheep, you know. They don't need any more putdowns."

Even so, there were times during his ministry when he was ready to give it all up, but "the Little Reverend" would say, "Trago, the Lord did not call you to give up." Trago would go in the prayer closet and ask forgiveness and go out again revived. By the term "Little Reverend", Trago was never indicating less of a status for his darling wife; rather he was whimsically referring to her tiny stature.

Margaret summed up the key to their successful union succinctly. "We loved each other and Christ." That commitment carried them together joyously for nearly five decades until Trago died on December 26, 1986 – just two days short of their 55th Wedding Anniversary.

"Mother Margaret" finally gave up teaching a Sunday school class at age seventy-five. "To give others a chance to serve," she said. But for years she continued to take delight in playing the organ for worship services. At 95, however, she had to lay that pleasure aside as she moved from her home just south of the church to live more comfortably and with continual care at Tabitha. For more than 20 years after the death of her husband she served as a faithful and loving matriarch for the tree that he so faithfully established.

Mother Margaret at Organ

Her favorite portion of Scripture is what the Lord Jesus Christ promised his disciples in John 14:2-3. "In my Father's house are many rooms; if it were no so, I would have told you. I am going there to prepare a place for you. And I if I go and prepare a place for you. I will come back and take you to be with me that you also may be where I am."

When asked why that was her favorite, she responded with a shy smile of assurance, "Because that is what I look forward to." Sister Margaret passed into Glory in 2009 at the age of 99. Heaven's gain was Lincoln's loss.

CHAPTER FOUR

A Ministry of Practical Service

Rev Kendall & Theresa McWilliams

Following the death of Trago, his first cousin, Kendall McWilliams became the Senior Pastor at Christ Temple Mission. Ordained in 1955, Kendall became an assistant to Trago in 1972. He served the church in many capacities and considered himself more of a teacher than preacher and preferred to work behind the scenes. But following the beloved pastor's death in 1986, Kendall realized he had the responsibility to be a calming presence in a period of transition. The congregation rallied around him and he became the new father figure for the church family.

Kendall's spiritual roots were deeply planted in the church. His maternal grandfather, William H. Vanderzee, co-founded the Christian Mission Church along with his (and Trago's) paternal grandparents, John and Sarah McWilliams in 1896.

His maternal great grandmother Ruth Cox Adams, who was born on December 18, 1818, was born in Tuckahoe, Talbot County, Maryland. She was a house slave and nurse in the home of Fitzhugh Lee (a relative of General Robert E. Lee), and the daughters in the home taught her to read and write. When she was 21, Ruth escaped, and about a year later, when she met Frederick Douglass, he immediately thought she was his sister, Harriet. Frederick had been raised on the Lloyd Plantation in Talbot County and was separated from Harriet and the rest of his siblings in 1838 when he had escaped. As they talked, he realized that Ruth was not his sister, but he invited her to come to Lynn, Massachusetts, and live in his home as his adopted sister. The man who arguably did more in the cause of the abolition of slavery than any other black man in the 19th Century had a close, endearing relationship with Ruth, whom he referred to as Harriet.

Ruth traveled via the Underground Railway which was planned and operated by Quakers. She stayed with the Douglass family for five years (1842-1847), and went by the name, Harriet Bailey. There she helped Frederick's four children and assisted in correspondence for his wife, Anna, who was illiterate. (To view some of the correspondence between Ruth and Frederick Douglass, see Appendix.)

In 1884, she moved to Lincoln, Nebraska with other family members. Grandma Ruth (as she was called) constantly assured everyone that God would make a way for them, while at the same time accomplishing the practical things that had to be done.

That same combination of faith in God and attending to the necessary matters of life, exhibited by Grandma Ruth, were the standards by which Kendall McWilliams distinguished himself. There were three things that mattered most to him: the Word of God, family relationships, and working with his hands. From the Bible, he received the necessary inspiration to give credence to everything else he did.

Working hard to provide for his family was a primary driving force in his life. He married Theresa Berry of Baldwin, Kansas on December 18, 1948 and their family grew to include six biological and two adopted children. All eight of them, spurred on by the encouragement of their parents, distinguished themselves in academic and athletic achievements. All of the children agree with the opinion expressed by the second daughter Karen who said of her father, "He was the kindest man I ever knew. He always thought of others, looking for ways to help those around him. He lived by the motto, 'If you can't heal, don't harm.'"

For the big man that he was, Kendall didn't push his weight around. His gentle spirit preferred the sidelines rather than the limelight. He lived in accordance with the admonition of James 1:19. "My dear brothers, take note of this: Everyone should be quick to listen, slow to speak, and slow to become angry."

He knew how to give a soft answer under the most difficult of situations. This gentleness was seen especially in his love for music. He could add beautiful harmony to any song he heard. He passed on his love of music to his children; in particular, his daughters spent countless hours singing and harmonizing together as a family pastime.

In addition to their eight children, Kendall and Theresa began opening their door to needy children in 1965. Over the next several years, a total of 90 foster children came to live with them; the most they had at one time was eleven. They came in all sizes and ages from infants to teens and races—Asians, blacks, Caucasians—a mixture similar to that of the membership of Christ Temple Church. "It is always a challenge," Kendall admitted at the time. But he added, in his own inimitable way, "We can do it because we don't know we can't."

In 1986 Kendall and Theresa were recognized for their efforts by being named the Great American Family of Southeast Nebraska by the Family Service Association and the Lincoln Association of Life Underwriters. (Nancy Reagan, wife of the President, served as the honorary chairwoman of the national awards program – for which the McWilliams's were nominated.)

Kendall & Theresa family photo

Kendall loved working with his hands, creating and building all sorts of useful things for the home and the church. When he became the welding instructor at the Nebraska State Penitentiary, he seized the opportunity to minister to his students. Within a year he had established a routine of leading the men in a study of the Bible, not only at the Penitentiary on Monday evening, but also at the Lincoln Correctional Center every Wednesday evening. His rapport with the men became legendary. Whenever he walked across the prison yard, men would stop whatever they were doing to wave or shout their greetings. In accordance with the teaching of the book of James, he did not show favoritism. He reached out to all men equally, even one like Charles Goodwin who has been in and out of prison three times said reflectively of Reverend McWilliams, "He is the first person I really listened to at the prison, and even though I was not a believer, he was like a dad to me."

At the time of Kendall's death, Harold Wilson, an inmate at the Penitentiary wrote, "There will never be anyone to fill his shoes. We are all better for having known him and now poorer that he has gone."

Even years after his death, men in prison still reverently speak about his influence on their lives. David Ware, an inmate at the Lincoln Correctional Center, said, "Reverend McWilliams taught us respect. If you didn't pay attention during Bible study, he would excuse you from the meeting. But he treated us with loving-kindness, like we were his son or grandson."

Kendall was an especially gifted teacher. His steady instruction in the Wednesday night Bible study gave stability and focus in the Word of God to the people who regularly sat under him at Christ Temple Mission. His greatest passion and joy was helping others understand the clear teaching of Scriptures.

He was forced to retire from teaching at the Penitentiary in 1998 when the government cut funding for educational activities for prisoners. For the last two years of his life, he devoted his attention to the work of the church even though his health was declining. Shortly after open-heart surgery he died of an apparent cardiac arrest early in the morning of July 5, 2000. Even as he lay dying, a woman whom he and Theresa had foster-parented decades earlier came to visit, still calling him Dad.

Leola Bullock, a family friend, said at his death, "He was always an inspiration to me because of his sense of justice, a person who practiced what he preached. It's a great loss because he cared for us, and he was one of the wisest people I knew."

Then Governor Mike Johann's movingly wrote, "While nothing can dull the pain of this loss for those who knew him and were close to him, we can be comforted by the knowledge that Reverend McWilliams' time on earth has left a legacy of love and generosity that could never possibly be forgotten."

CHAPTER FIVE

Giving Up a Fortune to Gain It All

Rev Thomas & Charlene Saddler

Christ Temple Mission searched for several months before asking Thomas Saddler, a man whom Trago had mentored, to assume the role of Senior Pastor in the fall of 1998, following the departure of Kendall

McWilliams. As Thomas assumed the responsibility, he meditated on the need for a vibrant church to have the right focus. "Let us fix our eyes on Jesus, the author and perfecter of our faith, who for the joy set before him endured the cross, scorning its shame, and sat down at the right hand of the throne of God." (Hebrews 12:2)

As a young man growing up in the troubled suburbs of Detroit Michigan in the 1950s, Thomas had the lofty ambition to make a name and a fortune for himself. There was, however, an obstacle obstructing his carnal plan. Most significantly, his mother saw to it that he was in church every Sunday. As a result of that steady influence he became familiar with the Bible and consequently knew that God had first claim on his life.

Meanwhile, most of his peers, attempting to stay alive were succumbing to gang pressure. Black political leaders were in such persistent pursuit of equal rights that they had little, if any time to give instruction to disenchanted youth seething with pent up rage and anger.

Nonetheless, Thomas stuck to a regimen of study as his primary means of advancing to a higher goal. He was the only black student in his class of 1965 who graduated as a member of the National Honor Society. Soon after he began his studies at Michigan State University, he was diagnosed with an onset of Multiple Sclerosis (MS). Though the news of was disturbing, it could not deter him from his ambition to become a financial success. Thomas had to leave school temporarily, but began anew at the University of Detroit under a program for the handicapped. As quickly as one door closed, another opened. Even so, he had none of his focus on what God's purpose for his life might be. Becoming a branch of a tree in Lincoln, Nebraska was not part of his plan.

After receiving a degree in Business Administration, Thomas began his career with the Sun Oil Company in Ohio. Two years later he was hired by Goodyear, which ultimately took him back to the more familiar area of Lansing. When a beautiful pre-law student came in to buy a set of tires, he made the sale and got a date. He and Charlene married two years later.

Meanwhile, the 1967 nearby Detroit riots were tearing the fabric of the city and state. Thomas didn't participate in the demonstrations, nor did he involve himself in meaningful dialogue about racial inequality. First and foremost, Thomas didn't want anything to stand in the way of his very personal mission for success so he remained silent. In his heart, however, he agreed with the fury of those bold enough to protest inequality in what was supposed to be the "Land of the Free."

In the 1970s, after being trained in Chicago to be a General Motors general sales manager, he was assigned to locate to Grand Island, Nebraska. Immediately it became clear that blacks were an unwanted minority. The dealership owner wanted Thomas to stay in the back room so he wouldn't "scare away the customers." After months of enduring blatant prejudice, he convinced the Detroit officials to transfer him to Lincoln. Thomas didn't express his seething anger, because he didn't want to jeopardize his plans to achieve financial success, but he had developed an inner belief system that "black was good, and white was bad." Fortunately, God had a plan for the young businessman bent upon storing up riches on earth.

Soon after arriving in Lincoln, Thomas met Trago McWilliams and immediately joined in the fellowship of Christ Temple Church. Patiently, the kindly pastor began to reach into the inner recesses of Thomas' heart, stirring quiet embers of faith back into life. His relationship with Pastor Trago soon revealed the folly of his racist standard that blacks were good and whites were bad. Trago taught that Jesus Christ is the only means of salvation for all men, and that love has no color and God has given each human life purpose.

This was shocking news to the young man from Detroit who had heard the ugly slurs and felt the disdain of racial prejudice all his life. Nonetheless, he had a yearning for a life that could make sense of it all. Within the fellowship of Christ Temple Church, he rubbed elbows weekly with whites, blacks, Native Americans, Mexicans, and an occasional Asian; and the love that motivated them all enthralled him. He came to the realization that Pastor Trago was right on target with his insistence that, "Jesus is the answer!"

After seven years with General Motors, Thomas was asked to join with other young executives in a "think tank" to devise ways of increasing sales. When it came time for him to share his thoughts, he spoke passionately about the need for people to be in tune with their spiritual nature. The response from the others was positive, which spurred him on to speak specifically about commitment to Jesus Christ, concluding with a bold invitation for those present to commit their lives to Jesus.

That proved to be one of the defining moments of his life. Ninety days later he was given the option – he could either resign or be fired. To preserve his clean resume, Thomas resigned and received only a meager severance payment.

God opened a wide door of witnessing for Thomas as a corrections officer at the Nebraska State Penitentiary. Housing more than 900 men, the institution was a hotbed of emotions and tensions. Never big in stature, and somewhat limited by his MS, Thomas was no match for the burly, rough and tumble inmates. But his quiet spirit, and love and concern for their best interests led allowed him to help many turn this lives around.

Meanwhile, within the fellowship of Christ Temple Church, under the constant direction of Trago, Thomas was learning the principles of being a servant leader. He often used the graphic example of Christ in John 15:4. "Remain in me, and I will remain in you. No branch can bear fruit by itself; it must remain in the vine. Neither can you bear fruit unless you remain in me."

Trago taught everyone under him the importance of a strong vertical relationship with God so that he in turn could be used horizontally to reach his fellow man. Although a gifted preacher, Trago encouraged others to become involved in pulpit ministry. He would have his associates take turns preaching.

Following in the footsteps of such leadership, with a proscribed four-year course of study, Thomas Saddler became a licensed preacher in 1985 and was ordained three years later. He had come full circle from his youthful desire to build a fortune for himself. Instead he had succumbed to the admonition of Jesus in Matthew 6:33. "Seek first his kingdom and his righteousness, and all these things will be given to you as well."

Prior to assuming the Senior Pastor's position at Christ Temple Mission, Thomas served as an Interim Chaplain for the Lincoln Correctional Center in the mid 1990s, where he was regarded as one of the best chaplains the institution ever had.

When he assumed the role of Senior Pastor of Christ Temple Mission, he was handed the task of assisting in the plans for rebuilding of the century-old church building, which was all but ready for the wrecking ball. Just as importantly, at this juncture in his life, Thomas realized that his own theological training had been limited, and committed himself to a prescribed course of study through the extension program offered by Concordia Seminary in St. Louis. Concordia's Ethnic Immigrant Institute of Theology allows students to do most of their studying on line with only occasional visits to the campus in St. Louis. His efforts took a big step forward on September 19, 2004 when he was commissioned as a Vicar at Christ Lutheran Church in Lincoln.

Several years earlier under Reverend Saddler's leadership, Christ Lutheran Church, at 4325 Sumner Street, had adopted Christ Temple as an outreach ministry and helped with some of the renovation of its historic building. For a while the congregation worshiped in temporary space at Christ Lutheran and later at the Malone Center until the project was completed. In time, however, the congregation at Christ Temple decided it wanted to remain non-denominational rather than become affiliated with the Lutheran Church.

Toward the end of 2005, Thomas left the pastorate at Christ Temple and continued on the ministry staff at Christ Lutheran while pursuing further studies. He graduated as a Lutheran minister in 2007, making him eligible to receive a call by a local congregation. Almost immediately he received such a call from the Unity Lutheran Church in Norfolk, Virginia. Today Thomas is retired and resides in Lincoln.

CHAPTER SIX

A Son of Thunder

Pastor Alan & Lori Jacobsen

When the Christ Temple Mission congregation moved back into their remodeled church building in 2006, it was a true spiritual homecoming. For Alan Jacobsen, who had overseen the remodeling process, the excitement was palpable. If men could restore the structural integrity of a 100 year-old building, he challenged others, imagine what the God of the universe could do in restoring the spiritual integrity to the lives of people in our community.

Although Alan had been away from Christ Temple Mission for a number of years, the church—known by its fruits of love and joy had remained close to his heart. As a young man, this church, comprised of many races and ethnicities, had been the ideal place of worship for his multi-racial family. In addition to four healthy sons of their own, Walt and Bonnie Jacobsen expanded their Danish family through the adoption process. First, from Holt International they welcomed Barbara from Korea; then from Lutheran Family Services, they adopted Melinda and Peggy who were bi-racial (African American/ Caucasian). Just as the Jacobsen's purposefully opened their hearts to these children, in like manner the church on North 25th Street was equally open to them.

The third of the Jacobsen sons, Alan, was at that time moving through the pivotal juncture of life – high school and beyond. He needed a foundation stone, not only to build upon but on which to stand secure as well.

Perhaps more than anything that attracted the earnest young man to Trago McWilliams and his teaching, was the fact that no one was shunted aside - everyone was welcome. This openness to others was in stark contrast to the attitude of many other church and community leaders. It's hard to say what pastor McWilliams' favorite verse of Scripture might have been, but he truly put John 3:16 into practice. "For God so loved the world that he gave his one and only Son, that whoever believes in him shall not perish but will have eternal life."

Pastor Trago understood and preached that Jesus' concept of "whoever" was all-inclusive, excluding no one who submitted their lives to the Lordship of Christ. Therefore, his vision of what the church should be was broad and extensive.

As he did with so many others, Pastor McWilliams took Alan under his wing and trained him. It was Trago's passion to help people identify their strengths, challenge them to set goals at a maximum level, and then provide them with opportunity to achieve them. He took to heart the admonition of Proverbs 27:23. "Be sure you know the condition of your flocks."

Alan Jacobsen
ordained by Pastor Trago McWilliams and Kendall

Consequently, while walking in faith himself, Trago maintained a watchful and encouraging eye on others for their benefit. Though he wanted everyone to give voice to what God was accomplishing in his or her life, his emphasis was on living it out in one's daily routine. Believing firmly that your life is your message, he insisted that it is necessary to keep the two in perfect harmony and sync.

Pastor Trago didn't throw such instruction around just to sound wise. On the contrary, he was a living example to the young men around him especially in times of conflict. His method was simple and direct. Speak with kind words and in a gracious spirit, being careful not to pull up the wheat with the tares. Nevertheless, he knew it was necessary to stand firm on a matter of truth, while committing its ultimate vindication to prayer. Trago never forgot that while you have to maintain order in the church, most of the battles we face are not of human flesh and blood - they are spiritual. He stood steadfast on this wise understanding of Ephesians 6:12. "For our struggle is not against flesh and blood, but against the rulers, against the authorities, against the powers of this dark world and against the spiritual forces of evil in the heavenly realms."

Because of this insight he was able to help people who were in disagreement with each other to take a careful look beyond their respective selves and see the conflict for what it was – an obstacle to the Gospel.

Part of his plan for building leaders was to turn the preaching over to others. On one such occasion it was Alan's opportunity. He threw himself into the moment and began his sermon in the same forceful manner that some ministers finish their message, full of enthusiasm and with an earnest plea for action. Afterwards, pastor McWilliams referred to him as my "Son of Thunder."

Alan liked the designation and continued to speak in that fashion. At some point, thinking that the young man was showing signs of pride in what he had to say, or in the way he said it, Trago drew him aside privately for instruction. "Make sure," he said, "that when the thunderstorm moves in, that it is not just noisy, but that it also brings rain." The admonition refined the would-be preacher's motivation. It was by that kind of careful pruning that Trago McWilliams made a lasting, positive impression on the men under him. His mentoring was not a one-size-fits-all approach, but rather was carefully adapted to each individual. He effectively emphasized the strengths, hopes, and desires of each person.

Nevertheless, he was not overly gentle. He was not hesitant in pointing out weaknesses and flaws. He was especially intent on countering the possibility of pride as cautioned against in Proverbs 16:18. "Pride goes before destruction, a haughty spirit before a fall."

In his homespun way, Trago often explained that if you have your nose in the air, you might drown during a rainstorm. His teaching was not just in his words—but more importantly, his life.

In the final analysis his preaching and teaching had a dual purpose. His intent was not only for the salvation of the individual but also for each person to extend himself or herself into the lives of others. He believed that a person should be active in the society at large, but never lose sight of the underlying purpose – to do the will of God! This is why he worked hard to develop community leaders with a faith-based directive.

However, many years after leaving CTM, Alan witnessed first-hand that many unfortunately bend the principles of faith for personal advantage—rather than allowing faith to influence politics, some allow politics to infect their individual faith.

But Trago's sterling example has served Alan throughout his adult life. Alan's desire to be active in the community led him to accept a position at Boys Town in Omaha as a Protestant Chaplain before leading him to Washington, D.C., the Middle East and back home to Lincoln. The small business that Alan and his wife, Lori, started over 30 years ago, now employs all three of their adult sons.

One of the greatest challenges Alan would face came during a time when he was the past State Chairman for a national organization that prepared voter guides for elections. When the information was brazenly partisan in smearing candidates from one political party, Alan challenged Christian leaders to put faith before politics and not distribute the guides. Pastors accepted the challenge not to allow politics to infect their faith or the faith of their congregants. The 150,000 targeted voter guides were discarded. It did not come without repercussions of men but Jacobsen remembered the mooring of his spiritual mentor, "there is no right way to do the wrong thing."

Trago's mentoring helped mold Alan's social conscience, and empower his level of commitment to get involved and use his talents. Several years ago, Alan and Lori helped with the construction of Lincoln Lutheran High School. A few years later, he played an instrumental role in helping legislation get passed which affects Parochial and Private Schools. (The Nebraska Secondary & Elementary Finance Authority Act gives private and parochial schools the ability to raise funds for building related projects tax free). Parochial schools have saved millions of dollars in interest due to this effort.

Often God uses one project to prepare us for the next. Alan's business and community service had equipped him to serve as building liaison and project manager for the Christ Temple Mission congregation in the restoration of the 100-year-old building. The structure was now reinforced with structural steel beams, the altar was redesigned and the basement turned into a "great hall" for meetings, classes and large events. At last the people were comfortably back in the building where decades earlier Reverend Trago McWilliams had welcomed people from all backgrounds to come together in worship regardless of their color, social/economic, or ethnic background.

Alan never expected that he would be asked to fill in as interim pastor following Thomas Saddler's resignation. But as providence would have it, Alan would ultimately serve as interim pastor before being asked to serve as Senior Pastor—a position he accepted in 2008 and served until November 2013.

Pastor Trago would be especially pleased that all three of Alan and Lori's sons—Justin, Mike, and Brad are followers of Jesus Christ. The fruit continues to grow on the vine.

CHAPTER SEVEN

Full Circle

Rev John & Charlene Harris

Charlene (Maxey) Harris literally grew up sitting on the front row of Christ Temple Mission Church. When her mother Joanne was involved with leading worship, she wanted to make sure she could keep an eye on her children.

From that vantage point Charlene, at the age of ten, had her first real encounter with Jesus Christ. Pastor Trago had preached a powerful message of salvation and the congregation began singing the soulful message of "Do Not Pass Me By:"

> *Pass me not, O gentle Savior*
> *Hear my humble cry*
> *While on others Thou are calling,*
> *Do not pass me by.*

> Chorus

> *Savior, Savior*
> *Hear my humble cry;*
> *While on others Thou art calling,*
> *Do not pass me by.*

> *Let me at Thy throne of mercy*
> *Find a sweet relief*
> *Kneeling there in deep contrition*
> *Help my unbelief.*

> *Thou the Spring of all my comfort,*
> *More than life to me,*
> *Whom have I on earth beside Thee?*
> *Whom in heav'n but Thee?*

Charlene didn't know the meaning of the word contrition, but she knew she wanted Jesus. When the kindly Pastor Trago knelt down to pray with the little girl, he asked her why she had come forward. With a tremble in her voice she responded, "I don't want Him to pass me by."

Not only did Jesus become her Savior that day, Charlene also committed herself to being an obedient servant. She especially looked forward to the second Sunday of each month, which was designated youth day - when the young people were responsible for the music, the teaching, everything. Church was a training ground for Christian service. Sister Margaret required her students to write reports on what they learned in Sunday School.

Both Trago and Margaret were hands-on in their discipleship of the young people. Charlene recalls that Trago knew how give a gentle rebuke when necessary. "Back when 'black power' was the byword, some of us girls were on the swings behind the church and shouting loudly back and forth to each other: "What power? Black power!"

Overhearing them, but not belittling their enthusiasm, Pastor Trago shouted out to them, "You had better be having some Jesus power!"

Though he was highly respected and honored by the youth of the church, still, sometimes they had their minds elsewhere. One Sunday night the service was about to get started when Aaron Maxey, Charlene's younger brother, asked Reverend McWilliams, "How long are you going to preach?"

"Why do you ask?" the Pastor responded.

"Because Aaron Maxey has plans," the boy declared.

Pastor Trago knew his flock. He shared their lives. It was quite natural many years later when Charlene fell in love with John Harris, a graduate of the University of Missouri, that they would ask Pastor Trago to perform their wedding ceremony. That was to be the last such occasion for Trago. He officiated over their union on July 26, 1986 and he entered into his ultimate union with God five months later on December 26, 1986.

Wedding of John & Charlene @ CTM

The Lord knew on that day, that down the road young John would become Senior Pastor of Christ Temple Mission. And he has prepared John throughout this adult life as a motivator and builder of people. Whether he's leading worship or speaking to individuals one-on-one, John has an ability to encourage and exhort those around him. In the tradition of so many who have been touched by Trago's ministry, John has often been used as a light in a dark world.

When Joann Maxey, Charlene's mother, a mighty pillar of Christ Temple Mission Church, died in 1992, there was an outpouring of love and appreciation for her life, and steadying support for her family. The church was packed full with mourners. In anticipation of that, her son-in-law John wired the sanctuary with cameras with extensions running to two television screens in the basement. Still there were others who couldn't get inside, but showed their respect for this remarkable woman by listening from outside the doors.

In 2007 Charlene, who works for the University of Nebraska in Love Library, came full-circle back into the heart of the congregation when her husband John became an associate pastor of the church. John brought a rich talent to the fellowship because of his own ministry of encouragement and outreach to the lost. In August 2002, he had founded "Encouragement Unlimited", which provides educational and motivational programs, which in turn offers hope and renewal through faith in a relationship with Jesus Christ.

In 1984 he obtained his bachelor's degree in radio, television and film production from the University of Missouri. Though he had experiences with Christ as a child and as a young man, John did not begin to follow Jesus wholeheartedly until 1986 – after he and Charlene were married.

For nearly eight years, he worked as the Special Assistant to the Vice Chancellor for Student Affairs at the University of Nebraska-Lincoln. John resigned his administrative position in 1998 in order to pursue God's call to live out his purpose. Since that time he has been a popular keynote and conference speaker, lecturing nationally in academia and to businesses on issues of diversity, cultural awareness, leadership, motivation and organizational effectiveness.

In 2014, John became the Senior Pastor at Christ Temple Church, after serving several years as Associate Pastor and several months as Interim Senior Pastor. He brings a breadth of teaching the Bible in the same spirit as that of Trago McWilliams. One man who listened to John speak the Word of God forcefully one Sunday said, "I never had the privilege of hearing Trago preach; but from what I've heard about him I would guess that John speaks with same powerful anointing that the founder of the church had."

John Leonard Harris in Pulpit

The church continues to proclaim the Gospel and declare the Love of God. And it continues, under John Harris' leadership now, to train new leaders. All four of John and Charlene's children—Preston, Shannon, Joanna and John Jr. are following in their family's legacy of faith in Jesus Christ and Him crucified.

CHAPTER EIGHT

Fruit Is Found on the Branches

Just days before He gave His life for the sins of the whole world, the Lord Jesus Christ gave a great lesson concerning trees. In dramatic fashion he showed his disciples that a tree is not just to stand tall and look pretty. Rather, it has a primary function and responsibility to reproduce. As told in Matthew 21:19-22, Jesus was walking back from the village of Bethany toward Jerusalem and he was hungry and saw a fig tree by the road, but found no fruit. "Then he said to it, "May you never bear fruit again!" Immediately the tree withered. When the disciples saw this, they were amazed. "How did the fig tree wither so quickly?" they asked. Jesus replied, "I tell you the truth, if you have faith and do not doubt, not only can you do what was done to the fig tree, but also you can say to this mountain, "Go, throw yourself into the sea," and it will be done. If you believe, you will receive whatever you ask for in prayer."

Certainly this is not only a promise to individuals but to the whole body as well. A church is not just to be place of beauty and splendor – one Saint Peters Basilica in the world is more than enough gold and refinement. Rather, the church is charged with the responsibility to reproduce – not just within its hallowed halls, but in the marketplace as well.

Toward the end of his Gospel account of Jesus, the Apostle John wrote: "many other miracles did Jesus perform, but these are written that you might believe that Jesus is the Christ the Son of the Living God and that in believing you might have everlasting life."

In that stead, we might say here, Trago McWilliams impacted more lives than those mentioned in this book. The personal accounts that follow were selected by the authors to provide a glimpse of the long-reaching effect that was born out of the obedience of one man to carry out the vision God placed in his heart.

In this sampling of faith-filled stories, it's clear that the love and grace that so characterized the lives of Trago and his wife, Margaret, was utilized by God to draw people to the transformational power of Jesus Christ.

Trago had a deep desire to proclaim the Gospel, and he did so faithfully from the pulpit, as well as his daily life, but he also equipped the saints to share their faith. Here are just a few brief accounts of lives impacted by Trago's teaching and mentorship.

-Art and Joan McWilliams-

Art & Joan McWilliams

There is no better example of this at Christ Temple Church than in the steadfast faith and witness of Arthur (Don) McWilliams, Jr. and his wife Joan. In 2004, Joan was the President of the Church Board and she played a vital role in the rebuilding project. She was instrumental in coordinating the combined efforts of members and volunteers. Art and Joan have diligently worked to maintain and restore the vision of their Uncle Trago.

Prior to retiring, Art carried his faith into the workplace with his responsibility of overseeing the food service for the athletes at the University of Nebraska. He was greatly influenced by his father, Arthur, Sr., a younger brother of Trago O. McWilliams, who worked for Burlington Northern Railroad in its Havelock shop. He echoed the sentiment of the entire church body when he said, "It isn't what we can receive, it's what we can give to make it better." Also, in regard to the inclusiveness of the fellowship, the elder Arthur affirmed, "We were taught to respect others, that it's wrong to judge other people by the color of their skin."

Joan and Art's leadership in the church continues to spread throughout the community. Art's expertise with food has been a great benefit to the church as he has helped develop the kitchen into a modern facility to continue providing ministry to reach homeless people and those in need. Like his Uncle Trago before him, he tirelessly challenges people and helps them find their gifts and talents—as an act of worship. He developed Tuesday & Thursday morning bible studies and encourages individuals to read Scriptures daily and pray.

Joan & Art McWilliams are like oak trees in the community connecting the past to the present—but maybe more importantly, connecting the present to the future. Their determination to equip the saints and develop leaders is a vital aspect of the current ministry.

Their combined knowledge of the community and the respect they garner from the community continues to provide what Trago used to remind us that we are the "*Salt of the Earth*." The impact they have on the community was demonstrated when their son, Ralph, passed suddenly due to a heart attack. The outpouring of the community was overwhelming—the little church on the corner of 25th and S couldn't hold all of the mourners.

The message that day was called the "*Covenant of Salt*." The Covenant of Salt not only preserves the vine but it nourishes and seasons the

Word that gives all of us the impetus and power to carry on. The vine continues to grow and the branches continue to bear fruit because of the cultivation of their faith and the salt they season the lives of so many.

-David Ford-

David Ford reviewing blue prints with Builder

David Ford's involvement with Christ Temple Mission signifies the importance of one person—to impact many. David had been a believer for many years and actively involved in ministry as president of the Lincoln chapter of the International Fellowship of Christian Business, as well as an active outreach to the Jewish people when he became an active part of Christ Temple Mission.

A couple of years later, it became evident that the building was structurally unsound and it was the responsibility of the trustees to decide on a course of action. The proposal to demolish the existing building and construct a new $3.5 million dollar edifice in its place was reluctantly favored by almost everyone. The plan would have provided the advantages that are commonplace in church facilities, but the loss of the historic building would have been devastating.

David was sure the best course of action was to restore, not destroy and replace the building. He was firm in his resolve, but wasn't being obstinate. Because of his expertise as a real estate broker in land management he knew something about buildings, so he asked experts to advise the church as to how the structure could be saved and be made useful.

Church bylaws stipulate that certain decisions (including building demolition) must be unanimous—so it was David's "one vote" that delayed tearing down the building.

David was very active in the day-to-day construction of the remodeling project. He was most notably the expert in making sure that everything that was paint-able received the right application. His fingerprints are all over the church.

-Mae Scott-

Mae Scott with Trago & Margaret

Mae Scott was the first Native American to be grafted into the Christ Temple Mission tree of faith. Born into a large family on the Rosebud Sioux Reservation in northern Nebraska, her father, a full-blooded Lakota Indian, was a medicine man for the tribe. (See Appendix for more information on the Lakota Tribe.) Her parents were also members of the Roman Catholic Church, which allowed native practices as long as they declared allegiance to the church. From the time she was only five years old, Mae was forced to leave her home for nine months a year to live under the stern conditions of the church's boarding school. The English language was the only acceptable way of communication, and any student overheard speaking in their native Lakota tongue was rapped across the knuckles with a ruler by the nuns.

Life on the reservation was difficult for many people, but Mae's family always had enough to eat because her Mom always planted a large garden and kept geese, chickens and turkeys. The geese and turkeys were constantly wandering off and becoming someone else's property. Her dad was able to borrow large sums of money in order to buy cattle and the hay to feed them.

After high school Mae married Joe Scott, and the young couple left the reservation and moved to Lincoln where Joe quickly found work. Soon their family was expanded to include a son and daughter. Mae felt a void in her heart, but she had turned away from the hypocrisy that she saw in the religion of her youth. In 1956, Pearl Harris, a white friend, began asking her to visit Christ Temple Mission "The people in this church love one another and are sincere. And the pastor lives what he preaches," Mother Harris assured her.

After weeks of prodding, Mae finally agreed to visit the church and was instantly amazed by the love and togetherness expressed in the racially mixed congregation. Several months later, Mae finally surrendered her life to Jesus when Pastor Trago preached from a message based on 1 Timothy 2:5. "For there is one God and one mediator between God and men, the man Christ Jesus." When Mae understood that truth, there was no holding back. Soon, Mae and her two children were baptized and she has been a faithful member of the church since then, and has served for many years as a deaconess.

One Sunday night, several months after her conversion, Mae commented to Pastor Trago, "You have only one son, Richard, and no daughters. I want to be your daughter."

The pastor threw his arms around her in an embrace and declared, "Wonderful!" Then he called his wife Margaret over and said, "This is now our daughter!" Her adopted parents, Trago and Margaret, each independently affirmed the relationship sometime later, saying, "I couldn't love you more if you were my own flesh and blood."

This unusual family relationship underwent challenges when Mae was faced with a difficult pregnancy. Trago and Margaret stood steadfastly with their adopted daughter through the ordeal, and Mae named the beautiful little girl after her adopted mother. Margaret later carried on the family tradition, and named one of her sons, Trago.

Mae had the joy of seeing both of her biological parents; first her mother, and later her father commit their lives to Jesus at Christ Temple Mission Church. Today, on any given Sunday morning, you will find Mae with her grandchildren and great grandchildren worshiping together. She takes seriously the promise found in the Acts 2:42. "This promise is to you and your children."

-Albert and Joann Maxey-

Albert & Joann Maxey

Moving from Indianapolis, Indiana to Lincoln, Nebraska in 1959 was a difficult transition for Joann Maxey. She was used to having access to retail and media outlets that understood her needs because the black community comprised 40 percent of the total population of Indianapolis. But in Nebraska's capital city, with a black population of less than two percent, Joann quickly found that necessities like cosmetics and hosiery weren't readily available at the local store.

She had little choice, however, about coming to Lincoln. Joann had married her high school sweetheart, Albert, before the start of his junior year in college. Albert had moved to Lincoln to play basketball for the University of Nebraska Cornhusker's, after distinguishing himself in high school as a member of the Crispus Attucks championship team. (The all black school was named for the first man to die in the War of Independence. For more information about Crispus Attucks, see the Appendix.) The Crispus Attucks teams of the mid-1950s were a power to be reckoned within basketball-crazed Indiana. The all-star Oscar Robertson, who went on to play for the University of Cincinnati Bearcats and then to the NBA, was the leader of the Crispus Attucks squad. Both Robertson and Maxey were later inducted into the Indiana High School Basketball Hall of Fame. (Albert would also be inducted into the Nebraska Basketball Hall of Fame).

Joann had graduated from Shortridge, another predominantly black high school, before being trained as a medical technician, In Lincoln, she chose to pursue life vigorously—soon she was pregnant with her first child. From their first days in Lincoln as a young married couple, they enjoyed the encouragement that emanated from Christ Temple Mission Church. Though there were several black churches to choose from, they were especially attracted to the way in which Pastor Trago enthusiastically embraced everyone regardless of race. The fellowship was still meeting in the small white frame building on Y Street and everyone was expected to help carry the load—from ushering to cleaning, to teaching and preaching, and putting their musical talents to use. Joann soon became the choir director.

She also distinguished herself as a community leader, even serving in the Legislature prior to her untimely death from cancer. Albert joined the Lincoln Police Department, commencing a distinguished career of 33 years on the force. He spent another six years after that with the Lincoln Public Schools before retiring completely.

But through it all Albert has been attached to the fellowship he and his young bride found at Christ Temple. He has served as Chairman of the Church Board, and is currently the Chair of the security ministry. After Joann's death, Albert remarried. In honor of Joann's excellent leadership as an educator and state legislator, Maxey Elementary School, which is part of the Lincoln Public Schools system, was named in her honor.

-Bernice (Bowling) Onuoha-

Obassi & Bernice with family

The transforming power of Christ's Love best describes the gripping story of Bernice Bowling, who was a young mother with five little children, when she first became an integral part of Christ Temple Mission Church. When she moved with her husband, Charles, from Texas in 1959, her life was about to radically change.

When she first attended the church, she was surprised to see people of all colors and nationalities worshiping joyfully together. Then, when Trago began speaking, it seemed that every word was directed at her. "You go to church Sunday and then turn back to whatever pleases you," the preacher declared. "You just play church and you can't bring a sinner man into the Kingdom like that."

Bernice was in real turmoil as she listened. While many in the congregation were saying "Amen" and "Preach it brother!" she was groaning inwardly. She was certain that somehow he knew everything about her, and was directing each and every word her way. What struck the young mother most forcefully was when Trago solemnly spelled it out for the congregation, "S I N will take you to H E L L."

It was Bernice's first time there, but she wasted no time in answering the altar call. When the pastor knelt down across from her, he put his hand on her head and asked her what she wanted to pray about. Without apology she began to pour out her confession to God. "I had a heart change!" she declared later. "I cleaned my spiritual house that night and when I got home I told my husband that things needed to change in our house too."

Even though her husband didn't share her commitment to the Lord or family, Bernice threw herself wholeheartedly into the activities of the church while raising her children. When she saw something that she or someone else could do to relieve the load from the pastor, she found a way to assist in implementing the idea. She really thrived on the central theme that Pastor Trago kept emphasizing, "If you don't have love, you don't have anything." Within the year she was calling him "Dad" and his wife Margaret, "Mom." And in a very real sense, they had become her parents looking out for her best interest. She never asked Trago for anything, but he would sense her needs and often come to her home with produce from his garden or groceries at a needed time. Eventually Bernice married Obassi Onuoha and the couple added three more children to their family.

One of the first women in the church to befriend Bernice was Joann Maxey. When the basketball star's wife saw her with five little ones clinging to her, Joann asked in amazement, "Are all five of these little children yours? "Yes," she declared proudly. JoAnn and Bernice would become very good friends and work together on many projects for the church.

Pastor Trago was notorious for giving people assignments to get them involved in the life of the congregation—and he saw that both

Bernice and Joann were natural teachers. The two friends worked tirelessly with Mother Margaret McWilliams in developing a Sunday School education program. Many of their Sunday School attendees are strong in the faith today—proving the truth of Proverbs 22:6. "Train up a child in the way he should go, and when he is old he will not depart from it."

Bernice served in many capacities over the years—including Church President for over 27 years. In 1964, she was instrumental in establishing "Anniversary Sunday" which was an annual church offering day for Pastor Trago who received no salary.

One of the most treasured encounters with Pastor Trago came some 27 after she first met him. On her last visit with him, he was radiant as he assured her that he had turned everything over to Kendall and Little Reverend (his favorite name for his wife, Margaret).

-Dee and Jake Kirkland-

Dr. Jake & Dr. Dolores Kirkland

Dolores Simpson started attending Christ Temple Mission shortly after moving from New York City to begin her graduate program at UNL in the fall of 1975. When Trago and Margaret discovered that the young coed, who didn't have a car, couldn't get back to her campus in time to eat lunch at the dorm, they issued a standing invitation for her to eat with them each Sunday after church. That same year, Dolores was introduced to her future husband and fellow New Yorker, Jake, on campus. Although the two didn't see each other for another year and a half, they were engaged in June 1977 and married by Trago in October of that year. The Pastor gave the couple invaluable advice that has served them well. He dispelled the notion that marriage was a 50/50 proposition and explained that it was a sacrificial commitment that would sometimes be 70/30, and sometimes 90/10. Dolores remembers Trago as a man who demonstrated how to be a servant-leader. "After potluck, it was not unusual to see him back in the kitchen washing dishes."

Raised in a Christian home, Dolores attributes her time sitting under Trago's leader as a period in which she solidified her walk with the Lord. "It was a time of reexamination and re-dedication. He was very influential to me." Dolores remembers Trago as hard working and wise. "He was a man of integrity and character who had lots of adopted children. I loved him very much." Dolores and Jake have two children, who grew up attending Christ Temple Mission.

Both Dolores and Jake earned their Doctorate Degrees from the University of Nebraska, and have been leaders in the community as well as the church. Dolores is a Guidance Counselor at Southwest High School, and Jake has been at the University for over three decades and serves as the Assistant Director of Career Services. Dolores believes that school is a ministry and that one must allow the Lord to open their eyes and ears to the needs around them. A concert pianist, Dr. Dee is chairman of the Worship Committee. She also actively counsels, and consoles the hurting and visits the home-bound.

Today, Dr. Jake serves as Church Treasurer, and he has provided a stabilizing impact in many of the bumps that the congregation has encountered along the way. Dr. Jake, as he is passionately known by everyone within the congregation, has been a financial pillar in the church. As a close friend of Trago's, he has a strong tie to the church's past, but an understanding and commitment for the vision to train and develop young leaders for the future.

-*Connie Casmer*-

Connie Casmer

As the oldest of six children, Connie Casmer had to grow up fast in Depression-era Chicago. The children, who had to share two pair of shoes, ran to the Rail Road yards on Monday and Thursday to gather potatoes that had fallen off of the rail cars for the family to eat. When she was old enough, she worked at a liquor store—one in which Al Capone had a vested interest. Along with other family members, she also ran numbers (which was legal at the time).

She first attended Christ Temple Mission while visiting her sister in Lincoln in the 1940s. But after she married, Connie accompanied her husband to military bases in Japan and Paris before returning to Lincoln. When she got a phone installed in her home, the first call Connie received was from her husband who was asking for a divorce. By this time, the hard working mother of four sons was a committed Christian. She lived around the corner from the church and Connie, who routinely held down three or four jobs at a time, raised her sons as a single parent.

For years, Connie was the church treasurer and her son, Joe, is quick to concede that he is an active member of the church he grew up in today because of his mother's prayers. He reminisces that his Mother knew how to put her prayers to action when it came to protecting her sons. In 1960, a peeping Tom was breaking into houses in the neighborhood. The unfortunate criminal happened to try to crawl through a window. Joe woke to discover his mother holding a knife and beating the intruder (who was stuck) over the head with a cast iron skillet. Then she called for one of his brothers to load the 12 gauge shotgun and stand guard until the police arrived.

Another way that Connie put her faith to action was in advocating for justice. When a University of Nebraska policy wouldn't allow her oldest son, David, to attend school as a Nebraska resident, she and Trago were instrumental in taking action and getting the unfair policy changed.

David graduated from UNL College of Law in 1970, and is currently Professor Emeritus at the University of Denver Law School. During his distinguished career, he played a major role in developing the Model Academic Assistance Program which is used in many law schools.

Trago consistently demonstrated to his flock the need to be engaged in the world—to take a stand for justice. Joe recounts that Trago was like a father to him and many others. "The only thing Trago failed to do was to teach me to swim," he fondly recalls. Joe remembers a segregated Lincoln when the Municipal Bath House was the only place that children of color could swim, and when black service men were not allowed to eat at all of Lincoln's establishments. "Trago lived through racism, but he welcomed everyone in the church and took many people under his wing and it didn't matter what color they were.

He continues with his assessment, "It wasn't always what Trago said, but how he carried himself. He encouraged me never to limit myself, but at the same time, he reminded me not to let my nose get to high because the rain might pour in."

-*Ruth Miller*-

Ruth Miller

At the time of this writing, Ruth Miller proudly proclaims that she is 89 years young. However, as a young woman of 33 attending service at Christ Temple Mission for the first time, it didn't appear that she would reach advance years. After spending months in the Old Providence Hospital in Lincoln, her crippled body was carried to the front row pew at Christ Temple Mission Church on February 3, 1957. Reverend Susan Wilson, who was Trago's Assistant pastor, visited Ruth's roommate in the hospital and reached out to the young mother of four.

Pastor Trago anointed Ruth with oil before praying for her. "I can still feel his hands," Ruth reminisces. "The Holy Ghost went through my body and I felt my knee and back strengthen. I was healed." The next Sunday, Ruth walked into the church and she's been walking into church services ever since. Ruth felt right at home in the interracial church. As a child in Pennsylvania, Ruth attended a Bible believing church that included a black family. She first witnessed the evil of racism during nursing school, when she was chastised by the Director of Nursing for visiting the father of the black family in the hospital.

Ruth, who is a retired nurse, recently received a commemoration for 54 years of active volunteer service to the prison population. For years, six women and four men faithfully ministered in the penitentiary. Eventually, the ministry expanded to other facilities like LCC and York as well. Ruth still ministers with fellow Church members—Albert Maxey, David Ford, and John Harris.

Ruth remembers Trago as a true servant of God. "He always was a working pastor, but he was there for the flock. The only time he was unavailable was Thursday night. That was his date night with Margaret, whom he called 'honey', and he wouldn't answer the phone."

-The Fruit Multiplies-

Paul admonished believers to follow Christ alone. When Trago went to be with the Lord in 1986, his greatest desire for Christ Temple Mission was for the church to continue and grow. Now, there are many members who are faithful followers of Jesus Christ who never knew him. The work of the Lord continues.

The Lord has a way of bringing people with various talents into the local church body. Christ Temple Mission is blessed to have many people who bless the church with their various gifts. Diana Buchanan, who is married to Joe Casmer, is the Church Vice President. She has a deep faith and is a great leader, bringing her professional management skills to help with church administration.

Brother and sister, Michael and Mary Cates, moved to Lincoln from Tennessee and each married individuals whose families are integral parts of Christ Temple Mission. Mike is the head deacon and he works with local groups to promote the role of fathers in the lives of their children. Michael's wife, Christina, serves as secretary of the Lay Leadership Board and their daughter, Mariah Cates, is a member of Trinity Praise. Mary's husband, Herb Fultz, has strong ties to the community and is a church history buff. Growing up, his family was active in the church and their family was close to the McWilliams family. He serves as a deacon and also plays bass with the Prayer and

Praise Team. Herb has a wonderful heart for the Lord—choosing to live in joy in the midst of difficult circumstances with his health.

Another person who is a walking epistle for overcoming hardship is Precious Perry. She recently lost the love of her life, Michael Perry to kidney failure. As a couple they were truly the salt of the earth. Precious continues to serve the Lord as the leader of the Missions and Evangelism Ministry at Christ Temple Mission. Precious' name is a reflection of her being. She is truly precious in His sight and shines brightly for Christ.

Mary Jennings' love for unwanted and abandoned children is unmatched and reflects the passion that Kendall and Theresa McWilliams so selflessly provided to our community. Mary, who is also the church secretary, desires to see every child grow up with opportunities for a fruitful life. She has fostered and adopted numerous children with great success. Her latest gift to the church includes a wide assortment of recipes from church members. *Feed My Flock* demonstrates the cross-cultural diversity of this church body.

Single mother Judy Kennedy came to Lincoln from New Orleans with three children and found a home at Christ Temple. She later married Leonard Hudgins who serves as a deacon and is chair of building & grounds keeping. He came to faith in Christ through the Christ Temple Mission Prison Ministry. Judy leads the Prayer and Praise team and her oldest daughter, Lameakia Collier, directs Trinity Praise—a Worship Dance Group and also serves as Christian Education Director for the church.

Marvie Sullivan, a single mom and grandmother, has gifts reminiscent of Mother Margaret McWilliams. Her commitment to the Sunday School program and Christian Education is unfaltering. She has a great gift for explaining and teaching the scriptures in simple terms. Marvie is also very involved in the VBS program.

There are so many others past and present who have served at Christ Temple. After attempting to pay homage to all of the believers who comprised the Hall of Faith, the Book of Hebrews author states in 11:32, "Well, how much more do I need to say?..." It's impossible to recount the stories of faith of so many who have called Christ Temple home over the years, but each one is known by God.

The tree continues to grow because the well-established roots found in the teaching and preaching of Pastor Trago have continued to be strengthened under the succession of leadership of Kendall McWilliams, Thomas Saddler, Alan Jacobsen, and now John Harris. The emphasis expressed by all these leaders of this small inter-racial, non-denominational church is to be an extension of Christ's love, grace, and mercy. Men in the pulpit can encourage and exhort, but fruit comes from the pews—from the branches.

Christmas Program 2010

Mother Margaret 99 Birthday

Hall of Faith

Wherefore we are surrounded by so great a cloud of witnesses, let us lay aside every weight and the sin that doth so easily beset us and run with patience the race that is set before us, looking unto Jesus, who for the joy that was set before him endured the cross and despised the shame and sat down at the right hand of the throne of God.

Hebrews 12:1-2

Hall of Faith

Christ Temple Revitalization
Ground Breaking Ceremony
November 16, 2003

Ground Breaking 2003

74

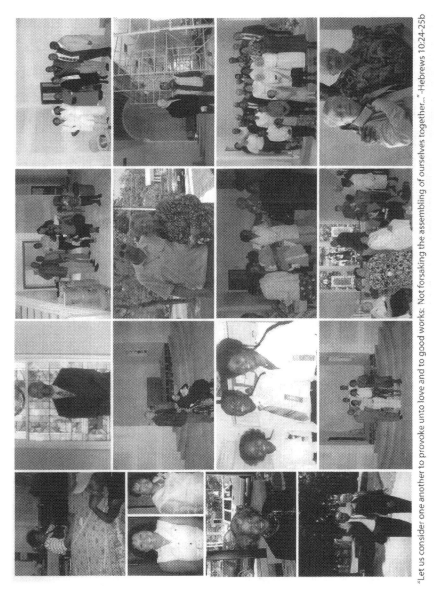

Fellowship of Believers

"Let us consider one another to provoke unto love and to good works: Not forsaking the assembling of ourselves together..." -Hebrews 10:24-25b

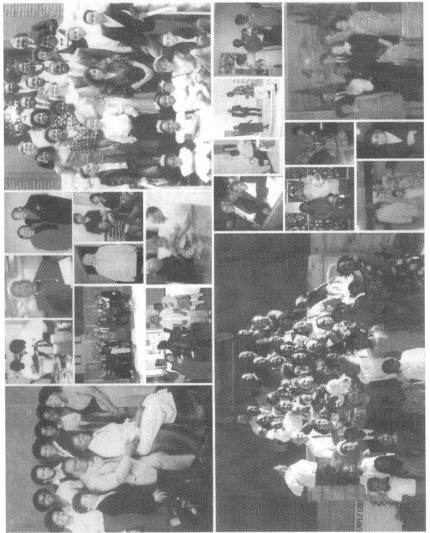

Fellowship over the Years

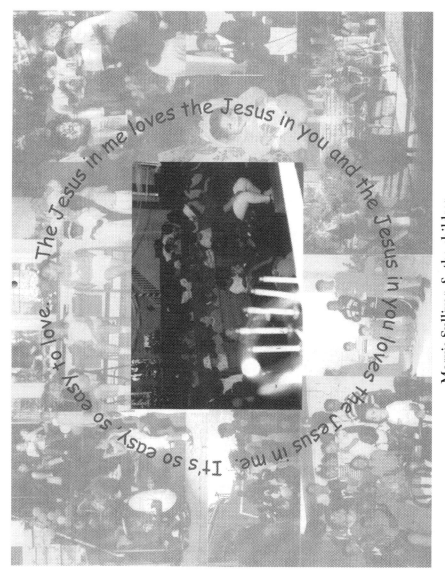

The Jesus in me loves the Jesus in you and the Jesus in you loves the Jesus in me. It's so easy, so easy to love.

Marvie Sullivan & the children

McWilliams Family Reunion August 1978

CHAPTER NINE

God Inhabits the Praises of His People

It's probably safe to say that everyone living within a 60 mile radius of Lincoln has been at one time or another impacted by music emanating from Christ Temple Mission.

Once while being interviewed by a newspaper reporter, Trago made it perfectly clear that not all black people could carry a tune. But, truly, whether one was musically inclined or not, Trago encouraged his congregation to live purposefully worshipful lives.

By all accounts, Trago was a man who lived his life as a praise-offering to the Lord. Alice Bowling Wirth, who pursued a successful career in academia, developed her leadership abilities as well as her passion for Christ as a young woman at Christ Temple Mission. She reflects on the impact Pastor Trago & Margaret had on their family life, "From the age of five, my family lived across the street from the McWilliams'. I remember Reverend Trago as one of the happiest men I have ever known. He was always bouncing down the street, greeting everyone with a bright smile and whistling."

The oldest of the eight Bowling/Onuoha children, Alice remembers enthusiastically going to Pastor Trago one day and sharing with him the need to include the youth in leading the worship service. What would come from this initial conversation would be what is practiced as Youth Sunday continuing to the present day. Her sister, Sue Bowling Hill, remembers that Pastor Trago wanted young people to experience the joy of ministry. "On specified Sundays, the young people were in charge, and we took ownership," she recalls enthusiastically. "It was our service." On those Sundays, the youth were ushers, readers, greeters, and even speakers who were approved by Pastor Trago.

The first youth speaker was Joe Orduna, a young man who was leading a fellowship at the University. Alice led the first youth choir, but eventually the leadership of the choir would be given over to the talents of her brother, Charles. One of the dynamic memories of the youth Sunday was when a famous local Jazz singer, Annette Muriel, led the choir into the sanctuary singing *It's Been a Good Day.*

Charlene Maxey Harris, who inherited a love of music from her mother, has great memories of being involved in the youth choir. Through the choir, the young people developed friendships with many teenagers from other churches when they would get together for choir groupings. There was no competition between the several small black churches. Rather, they connected often in joint meetings – even making bus trips to Omaha to join in the fellowship of Friends of Christ Church, led by Reverend John Orduna.

Christ Temple Mission became known as a house of worship. A group that emerged from the youth choir was an interracial trio called the Christ Templettes. Comprised of Sue Bowling, Debbie Scott, and Tracy Hillman and accompanied by Roger Hillman, the group was in high demand beyond the church walls. They were asked to sing for various occasions, including worship services, weddings, and funerals. The harmony in song was a testimony to the unity that can be accomplished among three different races of individuals proclaiming the Gospel message. This group was a reflection of Pastor Trago's commitment for the Bible-believing church to stand together in unity across racial lines. Mother Margaret, in preparation for her own funeral, requested that they sing a popular favorite of this group, *There's a Sweet Sweet Spirit in this Place.*

Choirs of Christ Temple Mission Church

81

Another group named HOPE, which was led by Joe McBee, emerged from within the congregation. The name was their message as they sang songs that drew people to God through Jesus Christ. One of their favorite songs was the old spiritual "Amazing Grace." They started out like the hymn with only piano accompaniment from Bruce Simon and Karen McWilliams slowly singing the first verse.

Amazing Grace how sweet the sound
that saved a wretch like me,
I once was lost but now I am found,
was blind but now I see.

The other instruments and vocalists joined in—Ronnie Douglas (lead guitar), Kenny Belcher (bass), and vocalists Sandy Moody, Debbie Scott and Joe McBee (who also played the tambourine). The group had several drummers throughout its history, but Steve Stubblefield (Third World Offorah) was the most prominent.

Hope sang regularly on Youth Sundays. Joe McBee was great at getting other young people involved in the service by prompting them to sing with the group occasionally.

One of the hallmarks of Trago was that he had a special gift for getting everyone involved regardless of their color or choice of music. Not only did he encourage groups to spring forth to go forth into the community, he was especially good at finding talent within the congregation. He discovered that Ruth Miller played the harmonica.

The development of Youth Sunday and the fostering of music in the midst of the Christ Temple congregation spread to the surrounding community. Christ Temple began to host youth choirs for a Sunday afternoon Sing Fest. This became a regular event that created a dynamic atmosphere for fostering youth participation in the Church by challenging them to discover their God-given talents.

Trago understood that the vibrancy of the church was dependent on fostering an environment where people could worship God, and care for one another. The fourth Sunday evening became "Family

Night" a time of fellowship and "breaking bread" together. Everyone was always welcome. Trago was emphatic that God's people are to be a joyous people who share in one anothers lives. Worship was a way of life to Trago.

Sue Bowling Hill remembers that Pastor Trago was a man way ahead of his time, especially in regard to prejudice and cultural differences. "He gave special attention to those with disabilities long before the Americans with Disabilities Act passed, she remembers. Sue, a registered nurse, was greatly impacted by love being the central theme of every message. The spark that Trago & Margaret's message of love ignited in the spiritual hearts of the church body fanned out far beyond the walls of the church into the greater community. For over a decade, Sue headed up the city-wide Gospel Workshop Choir, which was non-denominational and bi-racial.

It's probably not possible to fully document the impact that Christ Temple Mission musicians have had on the entire community. The church has continued in the tradition set forth by Trago and Margaret, and remains a vibrant House of Worship.

The late Les Meyer was homeless and in need of a bath when he first wandered into a church breakfast meeting. The once successful business and family man was bitter from life's circumstances, but he found love and hope through the church's ministry. After sever months, he gave his heart to the Lord and became a faithful member of Christ Temple Mission. One Sunday when none of the music leadership was there at the beginning of worship, he surprised everyone one when he went to the keyboard and began playing. After he passed away, his memory sparked an old fire for Christ Temple Mission to once again have believers and choirs from other churches to come together on a regular basis.

Today, Christ Temple Mission Church has many members engaged in leading worship. Dolores Kirkland, who serves as Chairman of the Worship Committee, is the pianist for the Prayer and Praise Group. Judy Hudgins, who is also the chair of the Deaconesses, is the team leader. Other members include Mary Fultz, Korine Yapp, Angie

Monroe, Marvie Sullivan & Barbara Banks who has retired from the group but still sings with the group on occasion. Maurice Hite (also known as Big Country), a transplant from Mississippi, plays the lead guitar. Although his father played with Blues great BB King, Maurice's desire is to glorify the Lord in his music. The bass is played by Herb Fultz, a deacon and faithful follower of Jesus Christ grew up with the McWilliams family. He is a faithful member of the church, who helps meet the needs of the congregation.

Another young group that sprang up is a dance trio by the name of Trinity Praise was developed by Lameakia Collier. The dancers are Kymesha Key, Madison Jennings, and Mariah Cates. Lameakia is also the Christian Education Director and the director of the musical Christmas Play.

Under the direction of Angela Pillow, the group Prevail is comprised of Junior and Senior High School students and young adults. The group which performs dance marches to Christian music performs in competitions.

Christ Temple Mission is a place for people of all ages to worship. Born in 1931, Reverend Samuel Wade moved to Lincoln from Parma City, Missouri. The father of five served many years as a Baptist pastor while leading several quartets. Known as Rev, this "retired" pastor is a blessing to the flock. He's known for his intercessory prayer, southern preaching drawl and his tenor voice. It's a blessing to hear him sing great hymns of the faith, often with Prayer and Praise.

Delores Kirkland remembers a precious time that Trago and Margaret played a duet. "Music was a huge part of Trago's life. He loved it, and as he and Margaret played *I'm So Glad Jesus Lifted Me* that day, he played with such energy. Perhaps, that is the lasting legacy of Trago McWilliams' life. He lived his life as a worshipful expression of the one who had lifted him.

Chapter Ten

Taking the Time to Build Young People

Omaha Councilman Franklin Thompson

Each person is uniquely created in God's image. Trago McWilliams was beloved by so many, in part at least, because he knew how to minister to the individual. Human beings were not cookie-cutter versions to

Trago. He truly saw the person and as a result was a father-figure and spiritual mentor to many young people. He was a natural encourager who looked beyond present circumstances—to what the person could become if truly submitted to God. Those influenced by Trago are dispersed throughout the country now. One of those young people that the late pastor vested much time into is now an Omaha City Councilman.

Franklin Thompson's roots stretch to South Carolina and Georgia, and beyond—to the Gullah People of the coastal region. These steadfast people live in small farming and fishing communities along the coast and on the chain of Sea Islands that are parallel to the coast. Because of their emphasis on strong community interaction, and the geographical isolation in which they live, these direct descendants of slaves from Sierra Leone have been able to preserve more of their African cultural heritage than any other group of Black Americans. They continue to use African names, faithfully tell African folktales, speak a heavily accented Creole language, and enjoy a rich cuisine that is based largely on rice. (For more information about the Gullah people, see the Appendix.)

Franklin's parents left the coastal plains of South Carolina when his father joined the Air Force. Later he was transferred to Offutt Air Force Base in Omaha when Franklin was a teenager. But it was far from being an ideal home. His father was an alcoholic and neglectful, and his stepmother was abusive and a "gamble-holic." The government-established projects in which they lived suffered under poor management, resulting in poverty of both the pocket and opportunity.

After they moved to a new military assignment in Colorado, young Franklin left them at age 17 and returned to Omaha. By his own wit and will he shifted around for places to stay - sometimes with the family of his brother's wife, while sometimes the couch of a friend had to suffice. He survived on a meager diet, making use primarily of the federal lunch program at school. Within his freedom to choose for himself, strangely enough, he even developed a habit of going to church - though at the time he didn't know what good it was doing him.

His senior year of high school was at the tough and tumble, old Omaha Technical School. Tech High was composed of poor black students, many of them high-risk and politically frustrated. The failure rate, predictably, was enormous. Nonetheless, the independent-minded Franklin had a yearning desire to succeed, to achieve something beyond the confines of the neighborhood. This was in stark contradiction of those around him, and was not looked on with favor by his peers. Earning high honors on achievement tests, he was referred to as a "white boy". And that was strong condemnation, since some blacks during the 1970s angrily considered any white man as a devil. Consequently, most of his friends "dumbed-down" on purpose so as to escape criticism.

Because of his determination to do what was necessary in order to achieve, Franklin was under constant ridicule by those around him. Nonetheless, he was resolute in his goal not to sink socio-economically. This naturally led him to conclude that college was a necessary road to achievement. Consequently, he worked hard at odd jobs to save money to go to college. This, unfortunately, is where his Gullah heritage "did him in". The Gullah people have an intense distrust of banks and so did he. The $1000 cash he had worked so hard to save was stolen in the summer of 1972. When he figured out who had taken it, and went after the man with a knife. Not only did Franklin not get this money back, but he was thrown into jail because of the altercation.

Ultimately the charges against him were dropped, but the angry, bitter young man had a new resolve to pursue his education in Lincoln. He had no money and was cold and alone, but he was determined to make a mark for himself. When he and another student represented Tech High School at the All-State Student Music Festival in Lincoln, Franklin was impressed by some of those singing. One of his new found friends—Charles Bowling who was a student representative from Lincoln High School invited him to Church on Sunday morning.

Franklin was totally unprepared for what he was to experience. Never before had he seen whites and blacks worshiping together. His hatred for whites had been fueled by the non-militant black nationalists (who wanted their own black-controlled way of life) on the one hand and the black intelligentsia (like Cal-Berkeley socialist Angela Davis) on the other hand. He determined that the whites had shut him out of a fair chance to succeed. "I thought whites hated me," he said.

Attending Christ Temple Mission immediately challenged Frank to rethink his position. He was especially intrigued by a lanky white Dane Alan Jacobsen, who seemed totally at ease in the blend of races. The two would become close friends.

The most pivotal relationship that God had in store for Franklin at Christ Temple Mission, however, was the pastor of the church. Trago McWilliams not only introduced him to a vital relationship with Jesus Christ, but also took him under his wing as a personal apprentice. Franklin recalls that Trago drew him aside and challenged him to live larger than the norm. Trago quoted the words of Jesus from the last sentence of Luke 12:48. "From everyone who has been given much, much will be demanded; and from the one who has been entrusted much, much more will be asked."

Trago never let the young man wallow in self-pity, but rather firmly, yet kindly admonished him. Franklin remembers his mentor's words. "You have a lot of stuff in you. All that has happened to you was for a reason. God can use it in your life if you will allow him."

During Franklin's five years in Lincoln, while pursuing his university education, Pastor McWilliams proved to be the greatest influence in the young man's life—both in politics and faith. He insisted that the would-be educator and politician must build on the one foundation for life, Jesus Christ, weighing each option for its own merits. "Trago's method was to encourage and challenge," Franklin observes "With his wise counsel, he would push you into a corner and then ask you how you were going to deal with it. It felt like love, but did it ever sting."

Franklin learned that sometimes standing for truth means one is standing alone. "The Lord Jesus Christ makes it clear in Matthew 7 that truth is seldom with the majority. You can have a crowd of 500 against you, but if only God and you stand together, all the 500 will fall," Franklin explains.

He observes that he was a beaten down young man in 1972 when he arrived in Lincoln, but that God had been ordering his steps since he was a child, and protecting him from countless temptations. "I don't know what life would be like if I had skipped those five years at Christ Temple Mission. The perspective I have in government and in the teaching of race relations at UNO is a direct result of Reverend Trago's teachings. They made me who I am today."

Having risen to prominence in the city of Omaha as both an educator and a politician (elected to the city council from a district which is 96% white), Franklin takes a reality check on his own responsibility and holds John 3:19 as an important verse in navigating in today's world. "This is the verdict: Light has come into the world, but men loved darkness instead of light because their deeds were evil."

Pastor Trago understood the costs of serving Jesus Christ, and he understood the need for the human heart to be regenerated. He would often open his Bible to Hebrews 6:9. "Even though we speak like this, dear friends, we are confident of better things in your case – things that accompany salvation."

Chapter Eleven

Perspectives From Another Tree

Rev Dr. Schnache & Rev. Saddler

No tree is a forest by itself. Nor is a local congregation the Church by itself. The Body of Christ is comprised of believers and followers of Jesus Christ representing many denominations. Sometimes a local church body is strong and has the ability to graciously tender assistance to others as expressed in Philippians 4:15-16. "Moreover, as you Philippians know, in the early days of your acquaintance with the gospel, when I set out from Macedonia, not one church shared with me in the matter of giving and receiving, except you only; for even when I was in Thessalonica, you sent me aid again and again when I was in need."

That is the perspective God gave to Rev. S. T. Williams in regard to Christ Temple Mission Church, when he was an associate pastor of Christ Lutheran Church. Not only is he a man of firm faith in Jesus Christ, but he is also a highly disciplined person, which might well be attributable to his military experience. (He still holds the rank of Lt. Commander in the U. S. Navy Reserves.) His intention is to do nothing without careful thought and thorough preparation.

For that reason, when he was invited to join the staff of Christ Lutheran Church in Lincoln as the Pastor of Mission Ministries, he thought it wise to first consult with other black pastors in Lincoln. He wanted to be in tune with the dynamics of the community before making a major career move. At the time, he was happily situated in Fort Wayne, Indiana and knew little about Lincoln.

One of the two ministers he contacted by telephone was Thomas Saddler, pastor of Christ Temple. Thomas, as well as the other man, encouraged him strongly to move to Lincoln, which he subsequently did. A bond of friendship ensued from that first conversation and grew constantly after Reverend Williams took up his position at Christ Lutheran Church. Neither man was aware of the far-reaching effect their association would have on the future of Christ Temple.

With his organizational skills, Reverend Williams built a three-pronged approach that was to be congregation led: care-giving to the local body, focus on international mission efforts, and reaching out to needs in Lincoln. In this latter effort, once again, there were three elements: a Latino Ministry, an African Immigrant Ministry, and an Urban Ministry. The basic approach was to share the Word of God.

Over a period of time, it became clear to Pastors Saddler and Williams that the call from Fort Wayne and their growing friendship had not been mere happenstance. Rather it was evident that God had put them together for the benefit of Christ Temple Mission. Foremost in that inventory was a building that was in major disrepair, for which the congregation had been struggling unsuccessfully for a solution.

Seeing Christ Temple as an urban partner, Christ Lutheran, with full approval of its Senior Pastor Luke Schnache, agreed to come alongside the smaller body for a partnership in ministry. Initially there was considerable discussion as to whether it was viable to restore the century-old Christ Temple Church building or tear it down and replace it with a modern structure. The overwhelming sentiment of the congregation was to restore the integrity and the beauty of the church building (at one third the cost of building something new).

Once that decision was made, Christ Lutheran Church offered rent free use of their facility without obligation during the restoration process. Christ Temple was able to remain a church family when their own facility was being rebuilt. To say that the Christ Lutheran congregation went the extra mile is an understatement. A team of 18 men from their midst, who had carpentry skills, built an interior wall from the basement to the roof. Had they not built the temporary wall, the main roof may have collapsed on top of the sanctuary.

Following a presentation by Pastor Saddler at Christ Lutheran, Tim Wentz a member of Christ Lutheran and a professor at the University Of Nebraska College Of Engineering approached Saddler. Tim told Pastor Saddler that the Durham School of Architectural Engineering and Construction could help the church.

Professors Tim Wentz and Charles Berryman proceeded to make the remodeling of Christ Temple Mission Church the project of 85 Juniors & Seniors for an entire year. Structural, electrical and mechanical feasibility studies were performed by the students. Project presentations served as the final exam. Of the twelve projects submitted, eight believed the church should and could successfully be remodeled. These studies became the impetus behind the decision to restore the building.

Another significant area in which this sister-church relationship benefited Christ Temple was for further theological training for Thomas Saddler. Pastor Saddler vigorously pursued the challenge of additional education and was commissioned a vicar on September 19, 2004. This was his first step into being licensed in the Lutheran Church, Missouri Synod, for which Christ Temple could proudly send one of its sons off to Virginia to minister full-time.

Christ Lutheran Church and Christ Temple Mission Church broke down denominational walls that divide the Body of Christ, and by working together, they not only restored the structural integrity of a 100 year-old building, but they helped reestablish the presence of a 100 year old ministry.

The actions of the two church bodies were a fulfillment to Jesus' prayer in John 17. "I do not pray for these alone, but also for those who will believe in Me through their word, that they all may be one, as You, Father, are in Me, and I in You; that they also may be one in Us, that the world may believe that You sent Me."

CHAPTER TWELVE

Reflections on the Practical Theology of Trago McWilliams

Excerpts from messages delivered by Alan Jacobsen in 2008

Reflecting on the Mentoring of Pastor Trago McWilliams

When someone enters the renovated sanctuary of Christ Temple Mission Church on North 25th & "S" Streets in Lincoln, Nebraska, they're met with the power of the Holy Spirit of God. The Lord alone deserves all Glory and Honor and Praise. He alone is the source of source of strength and purpose for the congregation.

This is a warm, inviting church body because they are followers of the Lord Jesus Christ, and either first or second generation disciples of Trago McWilliams. The vitality and authority of the Word of God that Pastor McWilliams emphasized is evident today.

I was ordained in the ministry in the 1970s and served as an assistant pastor under Trago McWilliams for three years. In 2008, I had the privilege of devoting three sermons to the topic of what I learned from this powerful man of God. What follows are highlights from those sermons.

Trago preached the true Gospel that attracts people of all colors and nationalities. He developed and cultivated an environment within the local church that reflected what God wanted His Bride to be. Trago realized early on in this struggle for true liberty, that if we were to be 'free at last, free at last', it would be God's Love that would be the ingredient that would bring us together, keep us together and mold us into that people He promised. Bottom line, the church was supposed to be the reflection of the Kingdom of God on earth.

Today the idea of blatant segregation seems impossible to comprehend. Yet within "the land of the free", our education system and military were segregated. Blacks were often denied access to certain water fountains, restrooms, and restaurants. The segregation of public schools in Topeka, Kansas was challenged in 1953, the year I was born. The Supreme Court's ruling in Brown vs. Board of Education (Kansas) was supposed to end segregation in public education. It was described as the doctrine of separate but equal in education. The court ruled that the schools in America (specifically in Topeka, Kansas) were definitely separate but they were not equal.

Tragically, racial separation was advocated by Booker T. Washington in 1895 when he addressed the Cotton Exposition in Atlanta, Georgia. In the speech, Washington advocated for economic parity for blacks at the expense of social interaction between the races. He talked about the importance of earning $1 in the factory at the expense of spending $1 in the opera house. He raised his hand into the air and spread his fingers apart and said, 'in all things social we can be as separate as the five fingers on our hand and economically we can be as together as the hand.' And in a mighty gesture he closed his hand into a fist. With that the separate but equal doctrine grew.

To say that the speech was well received by the white population is an understatement. Retired Governor Rufus broke with southern protocol and ran across the stage to shake Washington's hand. His speech was so well received that he was offered huge sums of money to go on a speaking tour. Instead he became the first President and Principal of the famous Tuskegee Institute. He was determined to develop the skills of individuals so that African-Americans would further their competitive edge in the marketplace.

Other black leaders like W. E. Dubois, however, challenged the premise of the speech. They were not willing to concede social segregation for economic parity. Nonetheless, the separate but equal rule prevailed in America. One of the tragedies of this doctrine was exposed in the Brown vs. Board of Education case. According to a psychologist, when given the choice, 9 out of 10 black children chose a white doll over a black doll. The psychological damage of this doctrine would take a toll on American society well after it was determined that schools were separate but not equal.

There was a significant difference between race relations in Lincoln, Nebraska a Northern city and those of the South. However—the church was just as segregated. Malcolm X said the South is like the wolf—you know he's coming directly at you. The North is more like the fox - he is going to sneak around and surprise you.

Trago McWilliams began addressing the fox by displaying the bold Love of God. What better way to address the differences between the races than by bringing them together on Sunday morning at 11:00? It's interesting that Trago very seldom talked about racism or segregation. Instead he talked about Jesus and God's Love for us and how that love can transform a life.

Trago's mission was to share the Good News. He was about reconciling the world to God through the preaching of Jesus Christ and he was determined that nothing could make a greater statement about God's love than for a congregation than to live their lives together. He embraced the teaching of Galatians 3:26-29. "You are all sons of God through faith in Christ Jesus, for all of you who were baptized into Christ have clothed yourselves with Christ. There is neither Jew nor Greek, slave nor free, male nor female, [Trago would add Black or White] for you are all one in Christ Jesus. If you belong to Christ, then you are Abraham's seed, and heirs according to the promise."

The theology of Trago McWilliams was not complicated. He believed that salvation pivoted on the death, resurrection, and ascension of Jesus Christ. Prior to Jesus' earthly life, everyone looked to the promise of God that a Savior would come. Since then, everyone who believes that Jesus Christ is Lord and paid the price for their sins through his shed blood is saved. Trago judged the merits of all of his sermons on this standard. It was his duty to uplift Christ so that men and women would want to follow him.

We should be judging our sermons on the same standard. Do our sermons produce new disciples or better disciples for Christ? Do our messages entice people to follow Jesus? Do our sermons equip disciples to carry out the work they were called to do? Do our sermons cause people to look to the cross? Do our sermons inspire people to live for Christ?

Trago did not preach a one-sided Gospel. He reminded everyone that if they were saved and their lives were transformed then they should demonstrate that they loved their brother. He would often quote 1 John 4:20. "If anyone says, "I love God, yet hates his brother, he is a liar. For anyone who does not love his brother, whom he has seen, cannot love God, whom he has not seen."

This two-fold Gospel is best described by the teaching of Christ as he answered the religious leaders of his day as to what is the greatest commandment in Matthew 22:37-40.

"Love the Lord your God with all you heart and with all your soul and with all your mind. This is the first and greatest commandment.

And the second is like it: Love your neighbor as yourself. All the Law and the Prophets hang on these two commandments."

These commandments are engraved on a wooden plaque which hangs on the north wall of the sanctuary above the parlor windows. The first describes our love and commitment to God and the second is our love for our neighbor. It's hypocritical to claim one without the other. We're deceiving ourselves when in fact, we are spiritually destitute.

The message of Christ crucified was the catalyst for Trago's ministry. In preaching the truth, people from all walks of life, no matter what color they were, or what side of 'O' street they lived on, or what their socio-economic nomenclature happened to be came to be part of a vibrant body.

Trago did not plant a tree in Lincoln in order to prosper from it. He did not receive a salary, nor has any pastor since received a salary. Trago worked full-time to provide for he and his wife, but the major effort of his life was to keep the church doors open as long and often as he could. He never lost his focus for the need of fellowship, believing that through such interaction it was possible to break down barriers and accomplish racial reconciliation. It was not enough just to come together, sing some songs, and preach a sermon. It was critical to have fellowship.

Trago did not openly disagree with Booker T. Washington; he recognized Washington had lived in another era. Instead he took a different bold approach. He knew that we needed to spend time together and that in doing so the barriers that divide races would come down. We had picnics and potluck dinners. It was a great opportunity to be together and let our children play together and grow up in an environment that would be reflective of God's Kingdom – a community within a community demonstrating the love of God in a fashion that was more powerful than any sermon he could preach.

He extended this ministry to the ones who could not come to church – the sick, the fatherless, and those in prison. Christ Temple Church has had many individuals maintain a ministry inside the prisons.

Pastor Trago consistently insisted to all who would listen, "your life is your message." And in one significant area of his life he demonstrated that simple life teaching by the love he showered on his wife, Margaret. There was no mistake; these two people lived their faith. Nothing could be a better example of Christ's love for the church than to see the leader of Christ Temple love his wife. Being true and faithful to his spouse was a living example of Christ's love for the church – His body. But the bigger than life illustration of their love for one another was not just about an example of something spiritual. Trago practiced what he preached. He was his message. He was a living example of what men should be. The way he treated his wife spoke volumes about what kind of man he was. He demonstrated to young men how to be respectful to their wives.

Many of us were not married at that time, but he didn't let this stop him from teaching us the principle of the ingredients of a healthy marriage. This was a message that required his life example as well as his words if he was to be successful in displaying that love for your spouse is often an indicator of your spiritual condition.

Trago's affection for Margaret was a pure demonstration of Christ's love for the church. If more religious leaders loved their wives in this manner, our marriages within the church could be transformed.

From the time of the first meeting of Christ Temple Mission the fellowship was free from denominational guidelines. But Trago never allowed such freedom to be mistaken as disorder. He was determined to resolve all conflicts through the Scriptures and by listening to the "still small voice" within each believer.

One time, prior to a Sunday morning service, Trago asked all of the worship team to come into his office to pray together. A man came in and told Trago that he believed that God had told him to preach that morning. In my youth, I wondered how this man known for peaceful resolutions would handle this. Trago looked at me, raised his eyebrows and said to everyone, "Let's pray together".

Trago then invited the man to pray with us in preparation for the service. We all knelt and began praying. After we finished praying, the man asked Trago when he would be preaching. With a warm smile, Trago responded, "Well, son, God may have told you to come and preach here this morning, but He didn't tell me that you were supposed to preach. And so at this point I am going to proceed with the message he gave me this morning."

I stood there stunned with admiration. Trago could have directed the man to the door, but he delivered the resolution with kindness and precision without hurting the messenger. He accomplished much more than resolution – he prevented hurting an individual or making this person feel anything but welcome and he set an example for all the rest of us to follow.

Trago certainly realized that you have to maintain order in the church community, but he knew that most of the battles we face are not of flesh and blood but rather they are spiritual. He often referred to Ephesians 6:12. "For our struggle is not against flesh and blood, but against the rulers, against the authorities, against the powers of this dark world and against the spiritual forces of evil in the heavenly realms."

Trago was quick to help people in conflict with each other to see past the other person and recognize the conflict for what it was – an obstacle to the Gospel and the ministry of reconciliation. Too often, friction experienced between parishioners in churches has nothing to do with doctrine or Scriptural accuracy/integrity, but rather personal differences. Trago was quick to point out that we need to accentuate what united us, and avoid those things that divide us – preventing the opportunity for divisions to grow needlessly.

He also emphasized the importance of forgiveness. We should be quick to forgive and careful not to judge, because we have been forgiven much. He taught that our judgment assessment should be confined to behavior and not personality. We were frequently reminded of the admonishment found in the second chapter of Philippians to 'consider others better than ourselves'.

Trago demonstrated a great sense of confidence in who he was in Christ. He was not as interested in protecting something he started as he was in protecting the Gospel, which is what Christ started. That is why he was never given to the old saying "that's the way we have always done it," and was never so entrenched in what he started that would not allow for changes in the methodology of presenting the Gospel without changing the purpose of the church.

The nearly miraculous way in which the historic building itself was restored is not about the founder of Christ Temple but who the founder lifted up – Jesus Christ. Trago would not have wanted his followers wearing T-shirts with his picture on them. There is nothing wrong with paying homage to those who have gone before us, we can learn from them. But if we fail to grasp the mission they passed on to us – as a runner passes off the baton in a relay race – then we have failed to comprehend the mission of this church and what Trago taught me and others who knew him.

The attitude of Trago McWilliams could be summed up in John's testimony at the end of Revelation; "Now, I John, saw and heard these things. And when I heard and saw, I fell down to worship before the feet of the angel who showed me these things. Then he (the angel) said to me, See that you do not do that. For I am your fellow Servant, and of your brethren the prophets, and of those who keep the words of this book. Worship God!" (Revelation 22.8-9)

And if Trago were here today he would say the same thing, "don't do that (lift me up) but rather worship God. May the humble spirit of the patriarch of this church be manifested in our Worship of the Lord God and Savior that he lifted up.

Benediction

"Therefore, my beloved brethren, be ye steadfast, immovable, always abounding in the work of the Lord, knowing that your labor is not in vain in the Lord." (1 Corinthians 15:58)

EPILOGUE
BY ART LINDSAY

Of greatest significance in the story of Christ Temple Mission is the number of branches that have grown from the original root of faith planted by John and Sarah McWilliams in 1896 and then revitalized by Trago O. McWilliams in 1940. That this little tree has survived through many trying circumstances can only be attributed to the nourishing sap from the original Tree of Life. "If some of the branches have been broken off, and you, though a wild olive shoot, have been grafted in among the others and now share in the nourishing sap from the olive root; do not boast over those branches. If you do, consider this: You do not support the root, but the root supports you." (Romans 11:17- 18)

Nonetheless, in order for the Lord Jesus Christ to sustain any ministry decade after decade, there must be a stalwart effort on the part of His disciples. Though the outreach of Christ Temple Church has involved men and women of varying ethnic backgrounds - and this book attempts to honor that - it is obvious that the McWilliams family was the primary resource in the past that God used.

Pastor Trago, in true humility, would discount that fact. But in the very sense that he would not willingly accept credit or praise, is the foundation of being a servant upon which Jesus has always built His church. "If you have any encouragement from being united with Christ, if any comfort from his love, if any fellowship with the Spirit, if any tenderness and compassion, then make my joy complete by being like-minded, having the same love, being one in spirit and purpose. Do nothing out of selfish ambition or vain conceit, but in humility consider others better than your selves. Each of you should look not only to your own interests, but also to the interests of others." (Philippians 2:1-4)

It is very fitting that in the near-north neighborhood of Lincoln the city has designated two areas of trees as living and lasting memorials to the efforts of the McWilliams family. The first stand of trees, south of the Malone Center, is where Christ Temple Church worshiped in a white-framed building. It was named Trago Park in honor of Pastor Trago T. McWilliams, who at the time of his death was an associate pastor of Christ Temple, under his son.

When asked to comment on the proposed change of name for the park, Rev. Kendall McWilliams wrote:

> *Because of an outstanding record of (both public and private) service to Lincoln, Lancaster County Community . . . in establishing a Standard of Excellence in leadership, fostering the interracial growth and harmony, so vital to the co-existence of people of divergent ethnic backgrounds in the City of Lincoln, Nebraska.*
>
> *I support and endorse any plan of action that: recognizes groups, or individuals who have made a contributing, sacrificial, and lasting mark, on our beautiful city of Lincoln, Nebraska. Trago McWilliams qualifies easily for such an honor, and will prove to be a continuing inspiration to any, and all, seeking ways and examples of men and women to live peaceably with each other; to the end that: "None is at a loss for opportunity for the freedom to seek out their soul salvation and search for happiness."*
>
> *Should Trago McWilliams be selected for a name of a local park, and historical information provided to those who are interested, certainly his labor of love, his life's work, will not be in vain.*

As one who also bares the distinguished McWilliams name . . . I am both humbled and challenged by the beautiful consideration that I too may share in something that is of great importance to the recorded history of our community.

Trago Park

Several years later a second, smaller park at 25th and T streets, was renamed McWilliams Park in honor of the entire McWilliams family. Formerly known as Passive Park, it was renamed at the urging of Tim Francis, who at the time was president of the Malone Neighborhood Association. "The McWilliams family members have been real leaders in the black community," he said. "We wanted to recognize and acknowledge that."

A great number of people, however, own a significant portion of the credit for what God has accomplished through "the tree" planted and cared for by many in the McWilliams family. For, just as in the recent years, Christ Lutheran Church stood in partnership with the believers at Christ Temple, there have been others who have offered encouragement and challenge.

Not least among them would be the pastor from Omaha who officiated at Trago McWilliams' funeral – Rev. John Orduna. As both men sought to serve God by establishing a church in their respective communities, they realized the benefit of joint meetings. Consequently, they frequently bussed their congregations to one town or the other.

And in the process they built a strong bond of friendship. "Trago was totally involved with people," Rev. Orduna observed. "His sincerity was evident in the way he preached – with enthusiasm – and often with a bit of a bounce. Yet, he had great respect for sacred things and found it impossible not to cry at a wedding."

"Hope" would also be an appropriate name for McWilliams Park because that is what the family and Christ Temple has offered the community for more than seventy years. It was not by accident that out of all the magnificent music that has emanated from the church on North 25th Street, the most memorable is that of the Hope Singers. A contingent of those musicians and singers still come together with that single purpose – to render hope to the listener. That hope surely is the lasting treasure of what Trago McWilliams preached and encouraged his congregation to share with the entire world – beginning in Lincoln. It is the eternal assurance of that hope which the Apostle Paul wrote of in Romans 15:4. "For everything that was written in the past was written to teach us, so that through endurance and the encouragement of the Scriptures we might have hope."

Not only did he embrace it in the Word of God, but he spoke more powerfully and significantly of that hope in his admonition of prayer in Romans 15:13. May the God of hope fill you with all joy and peace as you trust in him, so that you may overflow with hope by the power of the Holy Spirit.

APPENDIX

Letters Between Ruth Cox and Frederick Douglass

The earliest letter we have addressed to his sister "Harriet" in Douglass' own handwriting is from London dated May 1846. There were other letters from London and one from Belfast, Ireland. Always he asked that she read his letter to his dear wife Anna (who was illiterate) over and over until she fully understood his work.

A few loving words to my own dear sister Harriet. You will observe that I commence to write very plain. I don't know how I shall hold out; at any rate I think you will be able to read it. I'll try to make it so that you can without much trouble.

I write not because I have much to say, but because I guess you will be pleased to get a word direct from your Brother's pen. Do I guess right?

Not having introduced my letter let me say a word about my health. It is only tolerable. I never feel very well in the spring. I, however, feel as well this spring as I remember to have felt at any time in the spring during the last five years.

Harriet, I got real low spirited a few days ago – quite down at the mouth. I felt worse than "Get out." My under lip hung like that of a motherless colt. I looked so ugly that I hated to see myself in a glass. There was no living for me; I was so snappish I would have kicked my grand "dada." I was in a terrible mood – "dat's a fac!" O Harriet, could I have seen you then, how soon would I have been relieved from that horrible feeling. You would have been so kind to me.

You would not have looked cross at me. I know you would not. Instead of looking cross as me, you would have with your own dear sisterly look, smoothed and stroked down my feverish forehead and spoken so kindly as to make me forget my sadness.

You will be anxious to know how I got out of this predicament. Well, I will tell you. I went down the street and saw in the window of a large store an old fiddle. The thought struck me it had been so long since I played any that it might do me some good. You know when I get hungry for home I always play. Well I bought the fiddle, gave a trifle for it, brought it to the hotel and struck up the "Camel's a Coming" – I had not played ten minutes before I began to feel better and gradually I came to myself again, and was a lively as a cricket and as loving as a lamb. But Hatta, it is a terrible feeling and I advise everybody to keep clear of it who can and those who can't to buy a fiddle. They say music is good for insane people and I believe everybody is more or less insane at times. I feel very foolish when I come out of my fits of insanity. I mean my fits of melancholy – all the same you know. Do you ever have them, dear Harriet? If you do, just take down my old fiddle. I am sure it will do you good. Harriet, you were always so dear to me, but never so dear as now. Your devotion to my little boys, your attention to dear Anna, your smartness in learning to read and write and your loving letters to me have made you doubly dear to me. I will not forget you. What you do for my Anna and my children I shall consider as done to myself and will reward you with a brother's and father's care.

I am going on bravely with my Anti-slavery work. My book is selling slowly but surely. I have fourteen hundred copies to dispose of before I come home. I wish I could see my way clear to come home in July with my old friend and brother, James – with whom you may confidently expect to shake hands on the 18th of July. If I could sell what books I have on hand by that time I would come, but this I do not expect so I submit to my fate, and will try to make myself contented. The right way when we can do no better.

Read the enclosed letter, which I send to my dear Anna, over and over again till she can fully understand its contents. Remember me very affectionately to all who make friendly inquiries after me. Speak kindly of me to our mutually dear friend Mrs. Fletcher. Take care of all the papers, which I send. Look after my little trees. Kiss all my dear boys for me and believe me to be always your brother.

Frederick Douglass

In 1847, Ruth wrote her brother of her wish to marry, and asked him to be home for the wedding in Lynn, Massachusetts. She also asked him for a wedding dress. Her letter evoked a long response of surprise, bewilderment, advice, and a re-iteration of his real affection for her and best wishes for her future happiness. He also supplied the dress, from which she always kept a bit of its ribbon in her sewing box. That rosewood box with an intricate design in Mother-of-Peal on the top was also a gift from Frederick, which he told her about in a letter from Belfast on July 17, 1847.

My Own Dear Sister Harriet

I am not unmindful of you although I did not write to you by the last steamer. I always think of you among the beloved ones of my family. The enclosed letter is to my Dear Anna. I have written one, which will be read by Jeremiah. You will see both – and both of them I want you to read over and over

gain until Dear Anna shall fully understand their contents. I
shall not send any caps for our boys or a shawl for Dear Anna
as James has too many things to bring home for himself to be
troubled with mine. I shall send a beautiful workbox to you,
which I bought in London and gave six dollars for it. You will
be pleased with it, I know. The boys must wait for presents
till I come home, or until they come to this country. You will
get his letter about two weeks before you see friend Buffum.
Write me by the next steamer what you think of coming to
this country and spending a year or two. Speak, Dear Harriet,
just what you think even though you differ from me. I will
love you all the more for speaking out.

Your Brother, F. Douglass

Ruth did enjoy the happiness her brother had wished her in her marriage, and she had three children with Perry Francis Adams. After that, the paths of Ruth and Frederick widely separated - especially after he moved his family to Rochester, New York, and she moved to Nebraska. Totally unexpectedly, she received a final letter from her famous brother, written from his home at Cedar Hill in Anacostia, just outside of Washington, D.C., on March 9th 1984 – but addressed to her true name rather than to Harriet.

My Dear Ruth,

I have this day, through a Norfolk, Nebraska, newspaper
learned of your whereabouts, and am glad to find that you are
still in the land of the living. I went to Omaha in November
both for business, and largely in the hope of finding you. But
my search was in vain and I feared you had slipped away
to another world without my knowledge. I made diligent
inquiries for you, but nobody whom I asked could tell me
anything. I am now very glad to know that you still live and
have not forgotten what we were to each other in our younger
days. I am now 77 years old and am beginning to slow down.

It would do my heart good to see you again and talk over old times. Lewis, Rosetta, and Charley are living. Frederick died more than a year ago. Rosetta's head is now nearly as white as my own. She will be fifty-five years old in a few months. Rose and Lewis would be delighted to see you and I should be happy once more to see you under my roof and have you stay as long as we both live. I enclose this to your son-in-law, the better that you may get it.

Always affectionately yours,
Frederick Douglass

Frederick Douglass died less than a year after writing this letter in Washington, D.C. Ruth died in Lincoln, Nebraska at the age of 82 in 1900.

Among the many expressions of esteem for his life and time, was a twenty-five cent postage stamp, portraying Frederick Douglass issued on February 14, 1967, commemorating the 150th anniversary of his birth. The National Council of Negro Women bought and restored the Douglass home in Anacostia, where the public may see his memorabilia. The sewing box that Frederick Douglass purchased for Ruth is now the property of the Nebraska Historical Society.

THE LAKOTA PEOPLE

The words "Rosebud" and "Sioux" are actually not part of the Lakota vocabulary. Rosebud is the site name for the Federal Agency designated for the Sicangu People in 1877, so named because of the abundance of wild rosebuds that grew in the area. The term "Sioux" is an expression of derision (in the same way that early believers in Jesus were called "Christians"). It is short for "nadouessioux" or "little snakes", and came in the 1600s from the Chippewa, a longtime foe.

The U. S. Government officially recognized the Lakota as "Sioux" in 1825 and has applied this alien term to the Lakota, Dakota, and Nakota in official documents ever since. Over the years it has been widely adopted, even though the people of the Great Sioux Nation prefer to be called Dakota, Lakota or Nakota, according to the language group.

The seven original bands of the Great Sioux Nation were joined in an alliance called the "Oceti Sakowin," or "Seven Council Fires." This confederation of tribes spoke three dialects. The Santee spoke Dakota. The Yankton originally used Nakota, but many adopted the Dakota dialect in the mid-1800s. And the Teton spoke Lakota.

More properly known as Sicangu (Burnt Thigh), the Rosebud Sioux are from the Teton Lakota Band of the "Oceti Sakowin" (Seven Council Fires). The name "Sicangu", according to oral tradition, originated when a sudden prairie fire destroyed a Lakota village. Many children, as well as men and women, on foot some distance from the village, were burned to death. People who could get to a nearby lake saved themselves by jumping in. Many were badly burned about the upper legs from running through the tall, burning grass and this led to the name "Sicangu."

To summarize two hundred years of milestones in the Great Sioux Nation:

1800 - The Great Sioux Nation dominates the northern Plains, an area including most of the Dakotas, northern Nebraska, eastern Wyoming and southeastern Montana.

1803 - The United States purchases the Louisiana Territory from France. The westward expansion that follows eventually leads to the depletion of the buffalo, an animal central to the Lakota way of life.

1866-68 – Chief Red Cloud leads the successful fight to close off the Bozeman Trail, a pass leading to the gold mines of Montana. The trail crosses over the traditional hunting grounds of the Teton.

1868 - The Fort Laramie Treaty of 1868 establishes the Great Sioux Reservation, encompassing most of present-day South Dakota west of the Missouri River, including the Black Hills. The U. S. Government pledges to keep whites out of this territory.

1874 - Adventurers slip into the Black Hills and discover gold, creating a rush of prospectors to the area. As more and more white pour into the region, the native people defend their home and way of life.

1876 - On June 25, Lt. Col. George A. Custer attacks a large Indian encampment. Chiefs Sitting Bull, Crazy Horse, and several Cheyenne leaders defeat Custer and the 7th Cavalry at the Battle of Little Big Horn. Custer loses his entire command of more than 200 men in the battle.

1889 - An act of Congress in March 1889 splits the Great Sioux Reservation into six smaller reservations.

Some of the tribes begin performing the Ghost Dance, a religious ceremony thought to extinguish the whites, return the buffalo and the former way of life.

South Dakota is admitted to the Union in November.

1890 - Chief Sitting Bull is murdered on Standing Rock Reservation on December 15. Following this event, Chief Big Foot and his Minnecoujou band flee to Pine Ridge to seek protection under Chief Red Cloud. They are intercepted by the 7th Cavalry and brought, under a white flag of truce, to Wounded Knee. On the morning of December 29, soldiers prepare to search the band for weapons. A rifle is fired, setting off intense shooting of the mostly unarmed Indians, resulting in a massacre of more than 250. Most are buried in a mass grave nearby.

1924 - The Citizenship Act of 1924 naturalizes Indians born within the territorial limits of the United States.

1934 - The Indian Reorganization Act recognizes tribal governments as sovereign nations.

1973 - Members of the American Indian Movement seize the village of Wounded Knee and occupy it for 71 days.

1990 - South Dakota Governor George S. Mickelson and representatives of the state's nine tribal governments proclaim 1990 a Year of Reconciliation. A Century of Reconciliation is declared in 1991.

CRISPUS ATTUCKS

In the third quarter of the 18th Century, trouble boiled to overflowing for the British overlords as men and women in the American colonies began flexing their muscles in the yearning for freedom. Nearly everyone acquainted with that struggle can recall the details of the "Boston Tea Party" that struck back at unfair taxation in the week before Christmas in 1773. There was no loss of life that night, but that had not always been the case with the British. More than three years earlier, on the night of March 5, 1770, eight British soldiers fired on a large and unruly crowd. Crispus Attucks, at the head of that throng of people, was the "first to die in the American Revolution."

Since he was born a slave (about 1723), facts about Crispus Attucks are sketchy at best. But his heroism in facing down the British on the day of the "Boston Massacre" is beyond reproach. That bloody drama was but a skirmish in the opening of the pursuit by colonists in the cause for liberty – the War of Independence. (From a negative point of view some refer to it as the Revolutionary War. The attitude of most of the colonists, however, was more a cry for independence than a revolt against King George.)

Crispus Attucks' father, Prince, was born a freeman somewhere in Africa - but was ensnared by slave masters and shipped to New England to be sold on the auction block. In due time he married a Natick Indian girl named Nancy, who gave birth to their first child, Phoebe. Two years later a son, Crispus, was born.

He grew up a slave, laboring with his father on a farm near Framingham, Massachusetts, while his mother and sister did housework.

Reportedly, their master treated them with kindness and respect; but Crispus began to desire to be free. (Such an attitude likely came down from an Indian ancestor of his mother, John Attucks, whom the British executed for treason in 1676 during the King Philip War.)

Consequently, as he became too much of a problem, his master sold him. His new owner was more lenient, but it was not enough to satisfy Crispus. At age 27, during a business trip to Boston, he signed on as a harpoonist on a whaling ship. He knew that the whaler would not return to Boston soon, so his master would not be able to find him.

It is from a fugitive slave notice that the owner put in The Boston Gazette on October 2, 1750 that we have an accurate description of the man:

> 10 Pound Reward
> For Return of Run Away Slave
>
> Ran away from his master William Brown of Framingham on the 30th of Sept. last a mulatto fellow about 27 years of age, named Crispus, 6 feet and 2 inches high, short curl'd hair, his knees nearer together than common; and had on a light colour'd beaver skin coat, plain new buckskin breeches, blue yarn stocking and a checked woolen shirt.
>
> Whoever shall take up said runaway and convey him to his aforesaid master shall have 10 pounds old tenor reward, and all necessary charges paid. And all masters of vessels and others are hereby cautioned against concealing or carrying off said servant on penalty of law.

In the fall of 1769, Attucks, now 46, returned to Boston. His occupation made him particularly vulnerable to the presence of the British. As a seaman, he felt the ever-present danger of being "impressed" into the British navy – a practice all too frequently used to fill up a ship's crew. Also, he had an on land job as a rope maker. In that work he faced competition from British troops, who often took part-time jobs during their off-duty hours – and who were willing to work for lower wages.

On Friday, March 2, 1770 a fight broke out between Boston rope makers and three British soldiers, setting the stage for a later confrontation. Three days later tensions escalated when a soldier entered a pub, looking for work. Instead he found a group of angry seaman including Attucks. He left the tavern unscathed, but church bells began ringing throughout the town to call citizens to the town square. Attucks walked onto a platform in front of a large crowd and spoke briefly but effectively about striking back against the British – to fight for freedom. Anticipating trouble, Captain Thomas Preston called his Twenty-ninth Regiment to duty.

A group of about 30, led by Attucks, advanced on the customs house and began taunting the guard with snowballs, sticks and insults. Seven other redcoats advanced to the aid of the lone soldier. Attucks laid down a challenge to the troops to fight without guns. Suddenly, someone yelled fire and the soldiers let loose a volley of shots.

As he was struck by two bullets, Attucks was the first to die. Rope maker Samuel Gray and sailor James Caldwell also died instantly. Samuel Maverick, a 17-year-old joiner's apprentice, died the next day. Irish leather worker Patrick Carr died nine days later, and six others were wounded.

Attucks' body was carried to famed Faneuil Hall, where it lay in state with Caldwell until March 8. (Gray and Maverick were honored in their homes.) The town's response to the murders expressed the significance of the sacrifices these men had made. For the funeral service, shops closed, bells rang, and thousands of citizens from all walks of life formed a long procession, six people deep, to the Old Granary Burial Ground where the bodies were committed to a common grave. (This was done despite laws and customs of that day that regulated the burial of blacks.)

At the memorial service many speeches were given about the bravery of Crispus Attucks. The fact that he had not been treated equally but still had the desire and courage to fight for his country became one of the greatest inspirations for the colonists in the struggle that finally broke out in earnest six years later.

The poet John Boyle O'Reilly wrote of Attucks:

> *And honor to Crispus Attucks,*
> *who was leader and voice that day.*
> *The first to defy,*
> *and the first to die,*
> *with Maverick, Carr and Gray.*
> *It riot or revolution,*
> *or mob or crowd as you may,*
> *such deaths have been seeds of nations,*
> *such lives shall be honored for ay.*

John Adams, who was later to become the second President of the United States, reluctantly agreed to serve as lawyer for the crown, defending the eight soldiers. He put on a vigorous defense, reviling the "mad behavior" of Attucks, "whose very looks was enough to terrify any person." Adams described him as the self-appointed leader of "the dreadful carnage."

Whatever the true circumstances might have been, the officer in charge and his men were acquitted on the grounds of self-defense - which further inflamed the public. Patriots, however, used the trial to demonstrate that law rather than mob rule had been maintained in Boston, and that even the hated redcoats could receive a fair trial. In spite of what the actual circumstances might have been on that dreadful night, Attucks -immortalized as "the first to defy, the first to die," - has been lauded as a true martyr: "the first to pour out his blood as a precious libation on the altar of a people's rights."

In remembrance, citizens of the city observed the anniversary of the Boston Massacre in each of the following years leading up to the war. In ceremonies designed to stir revolutionary fervor, they summoned the "discontented ghosts" of the victims. Paul Revere created a woodcut of the incident, and the National Archives housed a painting by noted

New England artist Benjamin Champney in graphic depiction of the event. Negro military companies took the name Attucks Guards. And communities named schools after him, such as Crispus Attucks High School in Indianapolis, Indiana.

Black abolitionists inaugurated a "Crispus Attucks Day" in 1858; and in 1888, the Crispus Attucks Monument was erected on the Boston Common. (The first monument there ever to be paid for by public funds.) At the unveiling, speaker John Fiske called the Boston Massacre "one of the most significant and impressive events in the noble struggle in which our forefathers succeeded in vindicating, for themselves and their posterity, the sacred right of self-government."

THE GULLAH PEOPLE

In fact, rice played a pivotal role in the enslavement of the Gullah people. During the formation of the colonies, landowners discovered that rice would grow well in the moist, semitropical coastal area. But the American colonists, with their European background, had no experience with the particular expertise necessary for the cultivation and harvesting of rice. They needed expert workers. Tragically, slavery was the answer the white plantation owners chose to solve their dilemma. To accomplish their greedy goal, they were willing to pay much higher prices for slaves from the rice growing regions of Africa.

Usually when slaves were captured and brought to the Western World, groups were separated so that all ties to their past would be broken and the idea of a rebellion would be lessened. It was different with the Gullah people (sometimes identified as Geechee). They were kept together because of their ability to farm rice. Bunce Island, which is off the coast of Sierra Leone, had a huge slave trading fortress from which the enslaved individuals were transported in the filthy holds of ships to Charleston.

The climate of the Sea Islands was semitropical, and the slave owners had a difficult time adapting to it. The hot and humid conditions, however, did not bother the slaves because they were accustomed to the same climate in their homeland. There also was a high incidence of malaria on the islands, but this didn't afflict the Gullah because they were resistant to it. The slave owners found the climate disagreeable and the malaria deadly.

There was no eminent threat of the slaves escaping because of the remoteness of the islands, so the slave masters pretty much left the Gullah people to themselves. This laissez faire attitude allowed the slaves to retain their traditional ways of life and beliefs.

To be sure, the slaves endured hardship, abuse, and injustice under the onerous system of bondage. But there were a few things that set this group apart from other slave communities across the country. First, the tremendous size of the rice plantations and the amount of work involved led to the development of the "task system", a different organization of labor that divided work among the slaves. This gave the slaves of the Sea Islands a sense of independence and personal contribution, and an attachment to the land that slaves on the mainland did not have. Slaves of this "low country" took pride in having created prosperous plantations out of wilderness and marshland.

On November 7, 1861 – less than six months after the Civil War began – Union troops invaded the low country; and the Sea Islands of Port Royal, Hilton Head, and St. Helena quickly became Union strongholds. The former slaves of the Sea Islands, now free, were among the first in the nation to own their own land and to serve in the Union Army. The first school for free slaves, Penn School, was established on St. Helena Island, giving the Gullah a sense of empowerment that grew stronger through the years.

Today the Gullah still share many similarities with the people of Sierra Leone and the West coast of Africa. Their language is a type of Pidgin that is a combination of English and the traditional language spoken by the Wolof and Fula people of West Africa. The two groups of people - separated by an ocean - fish and grow rice, have the same folk tales, make the same baskets, have similar language and similar belief systems.

The isolation of the islanders from the mainland, with no bridges from the Islands until the 1930's- as well as the practice of the plantation owners to retreat to the mainland during the malaria season - helped to preserve Africanisms as nowhere else in the United States. Often there were only a handful of whites in a wide area. Consequently, large numbers of Gullah people were allowed to stay together and retain their traditional way of life. Also, each island was isolated from other islands; so the practices, beliefs, and traditions of the people was not as influenced by other African ethnic groups, or by Europeans, as elsewhere on the North American Continent. The end result is that these ties to Africa are stronger than those of any other group of African Americans.

There are various speculations as to where the term "Gullah" originated. Immigration records for this group of Africans list Angola, Congo, or "Congo and Angola" as the port of origin for many of them. Some historians have speculated that the term "Gullah" might have derived from Angola or "N'gulla" as it would have been pronounced. Perhaps, these historians say, the term "N'gullah" or "Gullah" may have come to mean any African of recent arrival.

Unfortunately, the encroachment of tourism and industry onto the Sea Islands has meant an end to their way of life for many of the Gullah. It began in 1950 when General Joseph B. Fraser purchased land on Hilton Head. (That name has now become synonymous with luxurious living and luscious golf greens.) His son began the development of resort plantations, and many longtime residents were pressured into selling their land and moving off the islands.

These "outsiders" have built a school system that caters to them. The non-Gullah teachers and administrators are ignorant of, and critical of, Gullah speech and culture - resulting in a cultural suppression of the Gullah children. Industrial pollution has spoiled some of the waters for harvesting oyster, shrimp, crab, and fish, making it necessary for many of the Gullah people to seek other occupations – often unskilled ones. "Progress" is eroding what had been a strikingly unique way of life for the Gullah people.